BREAKING THROUGH the Clouds

Dannie Gregg & Jeremy A. Walker

Copyright © 2014 by Danielle Gregg

All rights reserved. No part of this book may be used, reproduced, stored in a retrieval system, or transmitted in any form whatsoever — including electronic, photocopy, recording — without prior written permission from the author, except in the case of brief quotations embodied in critical articles or reviews.

All Scripture quotations are taken from *The ESV® Bible* (*The Holy Bible, English Standard Version®*) copyright © 2001 by Crossway Bibles, a publishing ministry of Good News Publishers. ESV® Text Edition: 2007

FIRST EDITION

ISBN: 978-1-939748-91-1

Library of Congress Control Number: 2014952798

Published by

P.O. Box 2839, Apopka, FL 32704

Printed in the United States of America

In loving memory of Cotton –
until we can be together again.

Table of Contents

Introduction 7
1. Laying a Foundation 9
2. Miracle of Babies 23
3. God Knocked; I Answered 37
4. Love of Church 49
5. A Tragic Sight 69
6. One Day at a Time 89
7. The Funeral I Never Thought I Would Attend ... 109
8. Grief, Love, and Moving Forward 125
9. Healing the Brokenhearted 139
10. One Year Later 153
11. Gone, But Not Forgotten 175
About the Authors 183

Introduction

When God tugged at my heart in 2010, I listened. I didn't know what God was or how I was even hearing Him, but I knew that I had peace when I obeyed. I was able to begin this process, because I had a husband who was far more spiritual than he or I knew at the time. Jordan has always been soft-spoken and kind. He has always been loving and generous, and after we committed our lives to the Lord, I was able to see him grow into a man who allowed his faith to guide him and take him to spiritual places that I didn't even know existed. It was because of this faith that we were able to fix our eyes upon Jesus and follow Him in spite of our circumstances.

We were both able to walk with the Lord through a hardship that I couldn't see coming and wouldn't have believed, even if I had been told ahead of time. God didn't just introduce Himself to us and move on to the next house, He came into our lives and made our home His home. The mercy and compassion that the Holy Spirit showed us in those moments were exactly what they needed to be so that we could walk through tragedy and praise God's name in the end.

    You may not understand and you may not believe this can even be possible, but I can tell you from personal experience, God is able to take you by the hand and carry you through even the darkest of places.

Laying a Foundation

More often than not, a journey begins where another ends. Though we don't usually recognize these changes, we are often concluding and birthing new adventures throughout our lives. I was not aware that my life was changing when I met Jordan, and I never knew that I could walk where Jesus would eventually call me. In fact, I never really knew what walking with Jesus even was, but that is the beauty of a journey - you really don't have to know where you're going to be changed by every step.

Jordan and I met in 2006 when I was nineteen years old. Jordan was only twenty-one at the time, but already had a two-year-old son named Cason. Almost immediately, we became inseparable, even to the point that, after a few short weeks, I moved in with Jordan and Cason. We both worked full-time jobs and tried to make a life together as best we knew how.

Learning how to be a couple was a longer process than we might have expected. At first we had love, but that was about it. We were young, so we didn't have much in the way of money, time, communication, patience, or any of the other things you need to make a healthy relationship. In fact, when I look back on that time, I am amazed that we were able to stand each other at times.

In my early years, my mom had been in a very abusive relationship with my biological father. She wasn't allowed to work, wear what she wanted, or go anywhere without his approval. This kind of domination and devastating relationship was what helped to form a strong and determined spirit within my mother when she left him. I saw how she displayed this kind of strength and independence, and I equated it with freedom. I saw how my biological father had held her down, and understood why she would no longer allow anyone to make decisions for her. I never thought that such independence could ever play a negative role in my own relationships.

It took a great deal of determination to get out of the abuse she had been in, and it was primarily out of love for her three children that she left our biological father. My mom struggled to provide for us the year she was a single mother, but we never went without. There were times when she didn't take for herself so that she could give to us. I was attracted to this display of strength and dignity that seemed so natural to her. She showed me how a loving mother will sacrifice for her children.

Shortly after leaving my biological father, my mom met Kendel. He, too, had been in a previous relationship that left him both hurt and a single father. After Kendel married my mother, he adopted all three of us and devoted himself to being a great father.

I loved having Kendel around as my dad. He worked full-time and did all he could to help around the house. My dad didn't yell much; he was always so accepting and loving. He loved to tease his kids and was always up for a joke. He was sweet and patient and the one parent you wanted to come to school if you got into trouble. If mom showed up, you were dead meat, but dad was gentle. I don't know if it was because of the previous relationship that he had been in, or if it was the fact that he had already been raising a daughter, but there was something soft in the way he dealt with us. He knew the necessity of discipline and raising good children, but we would much rather be in trouble with dad than mom.

My parents made sure to remind us that we were siblings. Not step, no favorites, just brothers and sisters, equal. They expected us to treat each other as though we were flesh and blood and that meant a lot. We were encouraged to love each other as much as possible and see to it that our family was the most important relationship that we had.

Since my mom had been through so much, she gradually assumed the role of head of home in our new family. She made most of the decisions, planning, cleaning, etc. She was the strongest person I knew, who could work a full time job, run a household, and still find time to enjoy life. I often thought that a Super Woman Award should have gone to her.

The strength that I saw in my mother was something that I aspired to have. I wanted to be a strong woman and I wanted to be respected. Whether in the home or at work, I wanted people to know that I was in charge and I was not to be trifled with. I also assumed the role of decision maker when any opportunity was presented.

So when the time came to make decisions for Jordan, I was already trained to be the boss. I stepped in and made sure that my presence was felt. I was demanding and I barked orders left and right. Jordan was never to mention that I might be wrong because he would just get a lecture on how I was right. Even if I realized I was wrong, I would never let him know. I would either hide my mistake or blame him when it all blew up in my face.

At times, I even used Jordan's past for an excuse as to why he shouldn't make decisions. I loved Jordan, but I never saw him as a man who could make his own decision because he had already made so many bad decisions in the past. So even when I didn't really think my plan was the best, I didn't allow him to make a decision because there was no way I was going to trust someone else with my future. I was acting like his parent not his partner. Even in instances where I enjoyed what I did, I would never let myself think I was doing it to serve Jordan or Cason. I did it to improve their lives because my way was best.

For example, through the first few years of living together, the house was always a mess. I hated to clean the house when Jordan and I were there because I wanted to spend time with him - not cleaning. I did most of my cleaning when he was at work, but it would make me so mad when he would not pick up after himself.

When it was just Cason and him, he kept the house relatively clean, but after we had been dating a while, it was like he just expected me to start doing it all. Being the person that I was, I saw this assumption on his part as a shot at my independence. Also, when he cleaned, it was never really clean and I would have to do it all over again.

So my excuse for the house being a wreck every day was that I had to work to pay my own way in this world. I had to be an independent woman and there was no time at the end of a busy day to be cleaning some house. Besides, Jordan and Cason were the reason the house was messy in the first place. Maybe they should be the ones to clean it up. And hey, I was the pretty young thing that made the world go around for this man and his son. He should just be grateful that I lived in this busted old house.

(Maybe I wasn't that mean, but when I look back on things, maybe I was.)

At the time, Jordan worked on farming irrigation wells. This job was a great way for him to express himself and to get to work in an industry that suited him. He was outside all day and he loved to interact with the farmers he served. However, there was no real schedule that he had to follow. So my view was, if he was a little late to work one day, it didn't really matter because he didn't have some boss breathing down his neck about tardiness. So morning duty was all his. He could get Cason ready for school and get some breakfast made while I got my last little bit of sleep before work.

Also, I hated to cook, so I told Jordan I couldn't cook. That way he would cook dinner every night after he got off work. It was funny to watch him make us steak and potatoes for us, but warm up some mini corn dogs for Cason. Of course, being the decision maker that I was, I stepped in and told Jordan that Cason was old enough to learn to eat something other than corn dogs and mac-n-cheese.

After a couple of weeks of noticing the clothes Jordan picked out for Cason to wear to school, I knew I needed to save the day. I just couldn't take it. So I started to buy Cason's clothes and dress him in the mornings. The funny thing is, I really enjoyed taking care of Cason. He was so cute after I got done with him. Sleeves rolled half way up, his hair was cut and fixed, and I took him out of those hideous light-up shoes with cartoon characters on them!

At night, I started to give Cason his baths and realized he didn't know how to do anything but play in the tub. By the time he was four, Cason could completely wash himself. It made me proud to watch him grow and be independent.

To be honest, I think that the root of all this domination was that I didn't want to rely on anyone but myself. If I trusted someone else, or if I allowed someone else to make a decision for me, I might be hurt by that decision. Or worse, I might be under someone. I might be less than someone else, and that was something I was simply not willing to do. Even if it cost me the man I loved, I wasn't going to be walked on. Not by anyone.

I'm sure you are wondering what was wrong with Jordan. Why would he stay with a crazy control-freak like me?

In reality, he was the strongest one of all, because he was so patient with me during all this. Like me, he didn't know what a real relationship should be, partly because of the relationships he had in the past and partly because we were both so young and still trying to figure out who we were and even who we wanted to be.

I also think he was really thankful to have a woman

in his life. Someone who cared enough to pay attention to his child and someone he loved to be around. We really did love each other; we were just really bad at showing it.

Even though we had no idea how to be a functioning couple, we did know how to laugh and play. We could enjoy ourselves when we got away much better than when we were at home. For this reason, we looked for any opportunity to get out of the house, especially on weekends and holidays.

Jordan was a little redneck, country boy who liked to shoot guns off his front porch, drive circles around the house on ATV's or jump in his bronco to chase rabbits. He liked mudding and anything else that you can only do when nobody is around for miles.

Jordan had a knack for bringing home anything he thought was interesting. At one point in our tiny little backyard, we had a cow, three dogs, a cat, four chickens, and a goat. As odd as that may sound to you, it really became normal for us. I grew accustomed to discovering a new thing every week. I was really glad when the "treasure" he brought home wasn't alive, but the live ones tended to be the more interesting things we owned. He even liked hoeing weeds in the yard.

Weird, right?

I remember how he did this every summer night after supper. He would just grab the hoe and start stabbing at weeds in the yard while we talked, sometimes for hours. I really enjoyed those conversations. It was the only time I allowed Jordan to say what he was thinking and I really listened.

Jordan taught me how to shoot guns and I had grown to love it. He taught me to hunt and it was great fun to spend that time together. Jordan loved to do anything that seemed remotely redneck, so I quickly learned to enjoy them too.

When the weekend came, we would load up and visit family, go hunting, or anything else that made us feel free, but to be honest, church was never a part of that picture. We wanted to do the kinds of things that allowed us to let go of all the things that bogged us down, and quite frankly, the thought of sitting in a stuffy church and getting told how much of a sinner I was just didn't fit the mold.

We worked hard to be a family and worked hard to become the kind of people we thought we wanted to be, but we never felt like that old rent house was going to be home. It served as a shelter, it provided a place for us to return to at the end of the day, but it was never home and that's what we wanted. We wanted the kind of home that you never wanted to leave, the kind of home that made the stress of the day just melt away, and the kind of home where our kids, even though we only had one at the time, could grow. We wanted the home of our dreams.

But the home of our dreams was a little different

from what most people think. We didn't want a house in the suburbs. We didn't want a mansion on a hill somewhere. We didn't want that big city life. We wanted the kind of home that fit our personalities. We were a little different from most people and what we were looking for in a house would be a little different too.

Finding a home that was as unique as we were, as well as a place where we could be the people we wanted to be and live the lives we wanted to live seemed like a tall order. We really didn't know where to start, because there are so few places available in the area where we were living. The fact that so many of the existing homes are family-owned farm houses made it seem to be an insurmountable task.

So, in an effort to find the perfect home, we sat down and made a list of all the things we wanted in a house, so eventually, it could become our home. The list was almost like a penny dropped into a fountain. It was a wish upon a wish. It was almost like our own little "Happily Ever After" scenario. We thought if we could just get these things, we might stop fighting.

The List looked a little like this:
- Small community
- Outside the city limits
- Big enough we could grow into the house
- A little land where we could play
- A country feel without being too far removed from the convenience of the city

- And it's gotta have trees!

"Not a bad goal!" I thought.

The "trees" part was going to be hard to get done. We were in West Texas where trees only grow when you plant them, but I was undeterred! We set out to look for the wonderful home we had pictured in our dreams so many times before. We started in all the usual places. We looked in newspapers, periodicals, the internet, and contacted every family connection we had to try to find that perfect house, but after months of looking, we couldn't quite find what we were looking for.

We did find a house that met most of our goals and we even put in an offer. We waited and waited to hear back from the seller, but when we did, the news wasn't good. We were discouraged, to say the least, but we kept looking. We saw several other houses over the next few weeks, but nothing suited us. Nothing felt like home.

Then one day, kind of out of the blue, Jordan got a call from one of his grandmother's friends. Her name was Nadine and her family had been in the area for decades, just like Jordan's had. Nadine reached out to Jordan and told him that they were considering moving in to the city because of her husband's failing health, and to do so, they would have to sell their home. This home hadn't even been put on the market, yet and we were excited to take a look. We jumped into the car and took the short drive to see the house. As we drove, I tried not to get my hopes up, but I couldn't help wondering if we were driving to see our home for the first time.

We passed through the little town of Ropesville, Texas, and continued on the highway for another three miles. By the time we got to the house, we were only about fifteen miles from Lubbock, a city of almost a quarter million people. We turned off the big highway and crossed the train tracks to see a large brick house. As we drove across the three-acre pecan orchard, I was stunned to see two more giant mulberry trees in the back yard.

It was like someone took the list off our kitchen table and painted a picture of what I wanted. I was so excited to see the house, the trees, and the wide-open space, that I hardly heard Jordan mutter something about how nice the shop was in the back.

"Shop? Who cares about a shop when you have all these trees!" I thought.

As we walked into the house, it got even better. The house had two large living rooms that were separated by a wall of windows. The first bedroom we came to had wood paneling on the wall, and it had its own bathroom inside the room. The bathroom had a stand up shower, sink with a cabinet below, and toilet.

The second bedroom had white walls and was huge. I figured I could fit two twin beds and still have over half the room for playing. It also had a built-in window seat. I thought about how I could have someone make a cushioned seat for it. It would make a very nice reading spot. I could imagine our children laughing and playing in this room, even though we only had Cason at the time. I could hear their little voices and it got me even more excited.

This was an older model home, so everything had that look, but it had a wonderful structure and we knew we could make simple changes to make it our own. The carpet through the whole house, even in bathrooms, was white and didn't have a single stain. That made me nervous with these messy boys, but I just pushed the idea of grease and dirt stains to the back of my mind and focused on how beautiful this house was.

As we walked through the house, I was so surprised at how big it really was. Room after room and they all had their unique quality to them. Even the laundry room was special because it had two sets of cabinets, a large walk-in closet, and access to the basement, which was very small, and used primarily as a storage room and as a storm shelter.

The kitchen was moderately sized, but more than enough for our family. It had an island/bar that came off the fireplace, which separated the kitchen and the dining area. The dining area and the main living room were combined.

There was a back room that they called their sunroom. I wasn't really sure what a sunroom was used for, so I just called it our second living room. The sunroom had floor to ceiling windows all the way around. The only gap in the windows was the back door, which opened to the substantial yard.

In the back yard were those beautiful mulberry trees I saw from the front.

"This would be my office," I thought. "I will raise our children and it will be my favorite place to have them. I could just sit under these massive trees and enjoy the perfection of this place."

Jordan finally got me to come back inside by telling me that we still hadn't seen the master bedroom. I snapped back to reality and hurried back in to catch up with the others.

When I got to the master bedroom, I didn't want to leave. The master bedroom was twice the size of the other bedrooms. They had a king-size bed and a twin bed and a couch all in this bedroom and I could still make my way around. It had his and her sinks and closets. The bathroom even had a tub and shower that were separate. I was in a fantasyland. I'm sure everyone could see how much I wanted the house, so Jordan wasted no time and started haggling over the price. We arrived at a deal that made us both happy and I knew my search was over. I had found the house I wanted. All we had to do now was turn this house into our home.

Miracle of Babies

When Jordan and I were married in March, 2009, I was already blessed to be a mother to my stepson, Cason. I truly loved Cason and we developed a relationship that was unique. Our relationship began like you could imagine. At first, Cason was very protective of his dad. If I ever sat next to Jordan, Cason would come push me away and sit in my spot. He never really said anything about it, but you could always tell that he needed time to get to know me. He needed time to see if I was good for his daddy.

In an effort to begin to build a better relationship with Cason, we began to set aside time each day for just the two of us. Every afternoon, Cason and I would play while Jordan cooked dinner. It wasn't long until Cason would choose to sit with me instead of Jordan. On Saturdays, Cason started to go to work with me and be my little helper. After about a year of working on this relationship, during bath time one night, Cason called out, "Mom!!" I looked at Jordan, stunned because he had never called me mom before. He had always called me Dannie. So after the initial shock, I got up and went in the bathroom where he was.

"Why did you call me Mom?" I asked.

Cason said, "Because I wanted to. Don't you want me to call you Mom?"

I said, "If that is what you want to call me then I'd be happy for you to call me Mom."

Growing with Cason was hard, but it was a necessary part of making a family. Jordan and I knew that we wanted more children, so we had to start that process by building a solid foundation for additional kids. We didn't know the Lord yet, but we knew that the three of us would have to be a solid group of people so that we could encounter whatever came our way next.

We wanted a large family, so we were excited to start having more kids as soon as we could. Seeing that my relationship with Cason was growing, we wanted to take the opportunity to begin building on the family we had.

However, when I went to the doctor for my yearly checkup, my doctor explained to me that I had a condition called anovulation. He told me that it wasn't severe and that my life was not in any kind of danger as a result of it, but my chances of getting pregnant were reduced because the ovulation process was necessary for me to get pregnant.

I could feel the sting of doubt start to creep into my heart. I couldn't imagine my life without children of my own and the thought of that cut me deeply. I had wanted to be a mother for as long as I could remember.

I wanted to be the kind of mother my mother was to me. I wanted to invest in my own children with the same kind of passion my mother had for us. I wanted to give of myself so that they could have more and hopefully achieve more than I could ever imagine.

So, when I found out that I might not be able to have babies, my heart sank. I couldn't believe that I just got married and I had to tell my new husband that I might not be able to have kids.

Not yet believing in Jesus at that time, I didn't know what to do. I sat in my sorrows and just wished for a better outcome. I had no one to turn to. I wanted to change what was going on, but I didn't know how. All I could do was hope, but hope in what?

My doctor put me on birth control to get my body to ovulate. It's funny, as I look back, the way for me to get pregnant was to get on a pill that made it impossible to get pregnant. Nevertheless, I went ahead and did it.

I followed that regimen day after day, and day after day, I just had to trust that the doctor wouldn't steer me wrong. The process did not comfort me and I still felt very alone throughout the months. I began to hope that if and when I got pregnant, the child I had could be enough to fill the void in my heart.

After three months of birth control, my body started to ovulate normally. The doctors decided to take me off of birth control and start Clomid. Clomid is a medication that helps to ramp up the fertility process in women who have trouble getting pregnant. The doctors seemed so excited that my body had reacted so quickly to the whole process, that I had no doubt that we were only days away from announcing to our families that we were going to have a child.

But twenty-seven days later, I still wasn't pregnant. Depression was immediate, but I didn't let it stop me. I worked hard to not let the sadness take over and got myself geared up for round two of Clomid.

"Maybe there was still some of the birth control in my system," I thought. "I hope that this next go-around would be the one that gets it done." I could feel myself get excited again.

The days seemed to drag on, but twenty-nine days later, I still wasn't pregnant. I called the doctor to let him know that I wasn't pregnant. He informed me that I could only do six rounds of Clomid and if I still wasn't pregnant, we would have to try something different. I couldn't believe what I had just heard.

What was I going to do? Who could I turn to?

The thought of an end date on this medication was almost more than I could bear. What would we do then? If my body couldn't get pregnant to begin with, if regulating my cycle didn't help, and if Clomid didn't help, what would we do? I couldn't stand the thought that this wouldn't work. I had to stay focused. Keeping my eyes focused on the process was hard because the medicine wasn't helping. The process wasn't working.

All this time went by and Jordan, the strong, quiet type, was as supportive as he could be, but the fact was, there was little he could do to help. He never really came out and said it, but there seemed to be a calm assurance that, with enough time, the process would work, and we would have a child, but the fact that neither of us knew the Lord, the hope that he shared was just as weak as mine.

I could feel my discouragement and depression start to drive a wedge in between us. I noticed that we talked less and fought more. I heard myself become angry at little things and would speak so harshly to Jordan. I really became harsh and cold to everyone during those months, but Jordan was steady. Seeing him so focused helped me not to give up.

Round three.

After almost seven months of treatment and medication, I finally became pregnant. I could hardly wait to tell everyone the great news of our new baby. Jordan and I were overjoyed at the thought of having a baby together.

I enjoyed every bit of being pregnant. I worked so

hard to become pregnant; I wasn't going to let any part of it be negative. I tried to take every piece of advice I ever got and make it work for my baby. I had nausea for about two weeks, but quickly learned that as long as I snacked on something, I was fine. Plus, I was able to convince Jordan that I needed whatever food I craved because I was eating for two.

With each sonogram, I grew more and more in love with the baby growing inside of me and at twenty weeks, we discovered we were having a boy!

One day while I was working, I felt something crawl across the inside of my stomach. Having seen the movie Aliens, my immediate thought was terrifying, but after a few more flutters, I realized it was my baby moving. I can't even describe the awe of that moment. As the months passed, when I felt my baby move, I would stop and just soak in every moment. I would let people feel if they were around when he moved.

At the time, I worked a full-time job at a chiropractic office. I was the Assistant Manager and handled all the insurance billing. The job I was asked to do, along with the environment that surrounded me, wore on me every day.

My boss had a feeling that I would want to quit after having the baby, so she became even more difficult to work with. Negativity and stress began to grow within me, and every passing day, my work and my ability to be at that particular job became increasingly difficult.

Stress and anger at work continued to build to the point that we could no longer ignore what was going on. At 30 weeks, my blood pressure began to rise to a point that was not safe for my baby or for me. My doctor made it clear that I was going to have to stop cleaning the house, doing laundry, and most importantly I was going to have to quit my job.

All I could think was, "OH, NO! I can't be put on bed rest. I don't know if my boss will approve. She will be even more upset with me."

Jordan knew my fears of not being able to work, so he escorted me to the office to inform them of my doctor's decision. As I bawled like a baby, out of fear and worry of what they would say, I told my boss that I had to be put on bed rest.

My manager was stunned.

"Today? Right now? You can't finish the week? When will you be back? What am I supposed to do while you're gone? Well, I guess if that's what your doctors says, go home, but you will have to use this time off as your vacation time and you will not be paid for your six week maternity leave."

I didn't know what to say or think. I was glad that I didn't have to go back to work for a while, but the way that I was treated, even in that moment, made it difficult to relax. I struggled to be okay with being at home instead of working, but I continued to tell myself that it was good to be able to rest and help my baby grow strong in a much safer environment.

The first day or two of lying around was great. Although I was getting lots of rest, it drove me crazy how dirty the house was and I wasn't getting to clean it. The stress seemed to build as my work would call me to ask questions.

"Where's this?"

"Why is that done like that?"

"What does this mean?"

Half the time the answer was simple and it seemed like they were just calling for the sake of bugging me. It got to the point that I didn't just hate when the phone rang; I even began to fear it.

I was bed-ridden in every sense of the term. I wasn't allowed to do for myself and I was constantly being told to relax. How was I supposed to relax? I was working just as hard laying there as I was before.

Soon, I was hospitalized for the night, because of all the "rest" I was getting. The doctors monitored the baby and everything seemed fine, so I was told to go back to my doctor the following week.

At my 35-week checkup, my blood pressure was 200/100 and I was sent straight to the hospital for a procedure that would test my amniotic fluid to determine if the baby would be able to survive on his own. Something inside the amniotic fluid allows the doctors to know if the baby's lungs have developed to the point that he is able to breathe on his own.

Just the thought of having to go through another test made me stress even more, which wasn't good for my blood pressure or the baby.

What if I couldn't support him and his lungs aren't developed? What then? Doubt, fear, and worry do not come close to describing how anxious I felt in those moments.

After being admitted to the hospital, three or four nurses and a doctor walked into my room and began to explain the procedure to me. A needle as long as my arm would be inserted into my bulging stomach, while a nurse used an ultrasound machine to guide the doctor to my uterus without injuring me or the baby.

Easy, right?

What they failed to explain was how they expected me to just lay there and let this happen, or how they could keep my baby from flopping his way right into this giant needle, or how painful it was to have a needle poked into my pregnant belly!

All I could really do was hang on tightly to Jordan's hand and watch the monitor.

Jordan, on the other hand, was calm. He stood next to the bed holding my hand. He spoke very little and was gentle as usual. His calm demeanor was always such an encouragement to me. Some people may have found his unflappability to be unnerving, but I found that it calmed me. When beepers and buzzers and monitors and doctors couldn't seem to get quiet for even a few seconds, Jordan was always calm; he would just hold my hand and smile.

After collecting a sample, they slowly removed the needle. I'm not sure which hurt more, needle going in or out, but if they had taken any longer to get that thing out of me, I would have punched someone.

The physical pain began to subside, but the worry remained constant. The beep of the monitors and the periodical tightening of the blood pressure machine were constant reminders of how slowly time was passing. Every minute seemed like an eternity and few words were spoken because everything we had to say to each other rang hollow and dull.

After a few hours, my doctor came in with the results from the test. My baby's lungs were mature enough that he could survive on his own. It was best for baby and me if I went ahead and delivered.

I was terrified! I was not ready to have this baby! I didn't even have his nursery ready yet; I didn't even have our hospital bag ready... nothing!

The whole time the doctor was out, I just knew that he would come in to say that the baby wasn't ready so I would just go home for another week. I kept thinking that I didn't even feel like I had high blood pressure. I felt fine. I wasn't ready to deliver.

However, the doctor returned and let me know that it would be in the best interest of my baby and me that we deliver as soon as we could. We would make whatever arrangements we could in the next few hours, but this baby was coming whether we liked it or not.

The plan was set to deliver the next day. I would be induced at 6:00 a.m.

The next morning on February 13, 2010, everything went as planned. At 9:00 a.m., my doctor broke my water, and at 12:39 p.m., I delivered Colt Wesden Gregg. He weighed six pounds and nine ounces and was 19.5 inches long. He was the most beautiful thing I could have ever imagined. It took all I had to let someone else hold him. I never wanted to let him go. We had worked so hard to bring him into the world; I wanted to hold him forever.

I quit my stressful job to stay at home with Colt and the lack of stress helped us to become pregnant again. Six months after having Colt, we became pregnant. There were a couple of times we would get a scare about the progress of the pregnancy, but when I went in for an ultrasound, everything was fine.

We rode this rollercoaster of fear and relief over and over. The second child is said to be easier to have, but in reality, it was all the same. These two pregnancies were so similar that it was scary. The best part was that I didn't have to go to work in that office anymore.

Jordan would keep Colt while I went to all my doctor appointments, so he and Jordan grew very close. Colt loved riding on the tractor, or even working on the pump truck. He would just ride along in the car seat and stare at his daddy. Every afternoon Jordan would come home and spend time with Colt and Cason while I cooked dinner.

It's funny how our roles reversed by this time, but I can look back on it and know that it was the time we spent together that helped us build such loving relationships. I loved watching him play with his boys. I could tell that he was the kind of father that my boys needed and I was sure that this next child would love his daddy just as much as these two did.

On June 2, 2011, we were blessed again with another little boy, Cotton Lee Gregg. I had been able to go full term with no major complications, and our family seemed complete.

I was on cloud nine, having my boys and getting to be a stay-at-home mother too. Having children fifteen months apart is hard. They were like twins, but they were always just out of sync. Colt and Cotton were constantly at different stages in life. I was trying to potty train Colt and Cotton was into everything. I ran around like crazy trying to keep up with them, but we had a great time. We played and laughed and loved the time we had together.

As they grew, I couldn't help but sit and stare at Colt and Cotton. They were like two peas in a pod. They became best friends. Colt and Cotton did everything together, while Cason, our oldest, was at school. Always laughing and playing, they got into everything.

Once Cotton learned to crawl, he would follow Colt everywhere. Cotton loved when Colt played peek-a-boo with him. It was easy to see that these two would have a special kind of friendship.

Running through the house and around a laundry basket was their favorite pastime. It didn't seem to matter what the game was, they loved to play it together. They loved to giggle and make silly games out of everything they saw. As a mother, there is nothing more beautiful than the sound of your kids having a good time. I tried to cherish each moment we had, because one day those moments would be gone.

God Knocked; I Answered

*G*rowing up in a loving home, I never questioned what was right or wrong, but I never really had a basis for establishing right and wrong other than what my parents told me. I knew that I needed to do what I was told, but I had no spiritual basis for determining what I should do when I got older. It's not that I never went to church; it's just that we did it so little growing up that I never learned why people go to church. We went to my grandmother's church a couple of times, but all I could really remember from there was that the service was so long and the people were so old.

So when we got settled into our new home, before Cotton was born, I found it very odd that I started feeling so unsettled by the fact that we didn't go to church. My home was exactly what I wanted and I loved my husband and sons very much, but there was always something missing. Being newly married and new homeowners brought with it some discussions, arguments, and even fights about money, life, and love. We struggled to express ourselves to each other and even to know why such a little thing could turn into such a major fight.

The uneasiness that we felt seemed to be a constant in our lives and it seemed like I couldn't do anything right. I thought maybe the reason why I felt the need for a church was because it could help get my life in order. I had in my mind a picture of what church people looked like. I thought that maybe I could be around some of these people and their goodness could rub off on me somehow. I thought that if I could see how they lived, I might be able to live life like they did. Then, the arguments would stop. Then, maybe, I would feel complete.

I thought that the act of going to church could help us to be more of a family. I thought that maybe we might be able to be a part of a group of people who could help us be more together and at least look like we knew what we were doing, now that we were married. It might be that I was confused as to what a church really was, but I knew they had something I wanted.

So, we decided to go church shopping.

I say, "shopping" because that's what I thought. We'll take a look at a church, and if we don't like it, we'll go to a different one the next week. It'll be like shoe shopping and I love shoe shopping!

Jordan and I had gone to his grandmother's church a couple of times, but that was more to keep her company than it was about being at church. To be honest, I didn't even know how I felt about wanting to go to church because I had no intention on sitting in a church and learning about how many times a week I was screwing up my life by not obeying the rules. Even though I wanted to be in the church and learn from what the church had to offer, I didn't want to sit close enough to these perfect Christians that they could see how much my life was messed up. But the more I pushed the thought away, the stronger it became.

Jordan took the lead in the shopping, which I was unusually grateful for, and took all my church goals in mind as he picked our first church. My church list was a lot like my house list. The requests I had were:
- It had to be a smaller church
- We would only go for the morning service
- That service could only be one hour
- It had to be close to the house

I wanted to go to church; I didn't want to live there. I wanted as much of the church life as I could get without having to put much of myself into the process. I didn't really want my church attendance to change how I acted, or what I did; I really just wanted to improve the lives we already had.

Taking all my requests to heart, Jordan located a few churches in the nearby town of Ropesville. It was the closest town to our house, so it made sense that it was where we started looking, but the surprising thing was, for a town of a little over four hundred people, there were a lot of churches and they each had their own names. I didn't really question that I wanted to go to a Christian church, but I had no idea what "flavor" of church I wanted.

The thought of choosing the wrong church scared me even more than the idea of walking into a church in the first place. As my mind raced through all the possibilities that were ahead of us that morning, I almost gave up hope. But then I looked over at Jordan, and he was as calm as he could be.

"How can you be calm at a time like this?" I thought. My heart was pumping out of my chest and my mind raced with more fear and anxiety than I had ever had.

Almost at that exact moment, we turned into a parking lot and I read the sign for the first time, First Baptist Church. I immediately wondered what kind of crazy Baptist weirdoes were waiting on the other side of that wall, but we got out of the car anyway.

As we pulled Cason and Colt out of their car seats, I reminded Jordan several times, "If this church isn't any good, we're going somewhere else next week." And he reassured me just as many times that we could do exactly that.

As we walked up to the front door, I became

nervous that we had shown up too early. There were only seven or eight cars in the parking lot that morning and I feared that if we were too early, we would be asked a ton of questions about how perfect we were and I knew I didn't have the answers they wanted to hear.

I felt my nerves shake and thoughts flooded my mind: "Great, I have to sit with all these prefect people. I hope I can fool them so they think we are perfect people too. What if I know someone? What if they find out who I really am and what I have really done? Gosh, and preachers scare me the most. The worst part of church is listening to preachers get up and talk and yell and talk some more."

I tried to remember why I wanted to be there in the first place, but I was already there, so I just lowered my head and muscled through. As we found our way to the sanctuary, every one of the fifteen or so people in the building immediately came to greet us and hug us. I was surprised that they all hugged us and I couldn't decide whether or not I should stand there and enjoy the genuine love that I was feeling or run for my life.

Just as I was about to turn for the door, the preacher walked up and introduced himself as Brother Jimmy. I couldn't even look at him. I was so nervous and I knew he must have been able to see what a wreck my life was because preachers don't usually greet visitors at the beginning of the service. But he simply shook our hands and said he was so happy we were joining them.

Thankfully, the service was about to start so everyone left us alone and we found a seat. As the service went on, I was most impressed by the preacher. While the songs were being sung, he walked around and shook hands and hugged people.

I had never seen anything like this from a preacher especially during the church service. Most preachers were the kinds of people who never smiled, never acted like they were happy to see people, and usually had a way of telling you how bad of a person you were with every sentence that came off their lips. So to see this guy sincerely excited to see each person in attendance was startling.

Then it came time for him to give his sermon.

"Here we go. Now we'll see his true colors come out," I thought.

But yet again, I was shocked by what I saw. My nerves shuddered at first because I just knew he was aware of how much of a mess I was and how much I didn't belong in this place, but as he spoke my heart was drawn to what he said instead of being pushed away. I didn't even really understand all that he had to say, but I knew that I had never really heard it put like that before. I was hanging on every word he said and forgot to be scared for a few moments.

He never got behind the podium and you could tell that this wasn't just another talk. He didn't point his finger and yell at the crowd. In fact, I have never seen anyone preach this way. He stood by the front pews and helped us feel comfortable. He made the sermon interesting, funny, and kept my attention throughout the sermon. I felt the words come out of this preacher's mouth and shoot straight to my heart. Sometimes, I didn't quite understand what he meant, but I just had this feeling that I wanted to hear more, to know more.

When the service ended, I actually felt a little sad because I wasn't done enjoying the moment. I knew one of my requests for church was that it would only take an hour to get through, but I would have stayed longer just to get to experience more of that place.

As we made our way to the door, Brother Jimmy came to us to make sure we filled out a visitor sheet so he could pray for us and maybe come by to visit.

I had a hard time waiting until we exited the building to see what Jordan had been thinking this whole time. He just sat there with little visible indication of how he felt other than a near constant grin on his face. When we finally got into the car, I asked Jordan what he thought.

He said, "I think we will try that place again next week."

I was extremely excited about his answer.

A few days later, Brother Jimmy called to set up an appointment to come see us. To make a good impression, I made sure my house was spotless. I hoped this would help us to fit in.

The whole time I worked on the house, I was conflicted about trying to get myself cleaned up to see the pastor.

"Did I really have to do all this? Didn't he have to accept me however I was?" My mind raced the whole day and I was a little on edge by the time he showed up.

As I let him in, feelings of worry, shame, and fear came rushing back to my mind. "What am I supposed to say to this man? Or not say? Will he yell at me because I don't know anything about God? How stupid will I look since I don't know anything? Will he be disappointed? What if he is a cult leader and fills our heads full of crazy mumbo jumbo? I never even looked up what Baptist meant!"

We sat down at the table and Brother Jimmy asked a few questions about our lives, our church experience and expectations, and what we thought about Jesus. I didn't know much about churches or God so I was scared to even say the name of Jesus out loud. It was weird and uncomfortable to say the name Jesus, but Brother Jimmy is talking about Jesus and saying His name as if it was going out of style!

"What a weirdo!" I thought.

Until that point in my life, I had never met anyone who loved to talk about Jesus as much as this man. He had such a passion for the story and had such a gift at sharing the truth about my need for a Savior. I never felt bad. I never felt judged. I only felt that this Jesus had a plan for me and had made a way for me to escape the sadness and brokenness of my past.

As Brother Jimmy explained what it was to be saved, I didn't quite understand everything, but I had no trouble believing that it was true. It kind of helped me understand why I had that feeling of needing a church in the first place. It was hard to believe everything he said about Jesus and how Jesus loved us, even died for us, but I knew that if I was going to be saved, this was the only way it could happen. I realized that the only way that I was going to be healed from all the hurt that I had experienced and even inflicted on myself was to accept this Jesus and believe in the One who sent Him.

Jesus said to him,
"I am the way, and the truth, and the life.
No one comes to the Father except through me." John 14:6

I didn't need a new set of clothes; I didn't need to get new habits; I didn't even need a church. I needed Jesus. I had heard that all my life, but never knew what it really meant. So, I decided it was time I found out what it all meant.

That night, I asked Jesus to be the Lord of my life and Jordan did too. It was at this moment that our house became a home and that our church became our family. We had never experienced the kind of freedom that we had in Christ Jesus. I didn't have to pretend anymore; I didn't have to act like I was perfect; and I didn't have to morph into the Pine-Sol Lady anytime our church family was on their way over. I was free!

After we prayed, which was very weird and uncomfortable too, Brother Jimmy said, "So, when is the best time to baptize you guys?"

I thought, "Isn't that where you get dunked in water in front of everyone? This guy is crazy to think I am going to get in front of people to show them that at twenty-three years old, I haven't been baptized."

Fear of what other people would think of me rushed back in and I was about to blurt out, "That's for kids to do, not me!" But Jordan jumped in and set a date. I gave him a look like, "ARE YOU CRAZY!?!" He just grinned at me as if he knew what I had been thinking.

I hoped we would be able to be baptized without anyone really finding out about it, but as soon as our families found out that we were going to be baptized, they all came to watch. And even though I was extremely nervous to go through with it, the date was set, the family showed up, so into the water we went.

The feeling of the water rushing over my face then falling off was so amazing. It was the physical feeling of a new start. A feeling of hope. I came to realize why it was such a big deal. It was our new start to something wonderful. That day, I vowed to live this Christian life and walk with God like Brother Jimmy had taught us. The best part was, he wasn't just teaching us, he was also showing us by how he lived.

He lived this life and so did the rest of the church. They loved us and we loved them. We started to catch a glimpse of how valuable a church family really was and how important they can be to our lives. They began to show us that we didn't just choose Jesus; we also chose His church. We would need this church soon, and the fact that we fell in love so quickly only goes to show us that God was looking out for our future.

Love of Church

It was apparent from the start that something special was happening at our church. We "happened" to come here to visit and "accidentally" fell in love with what this church had to offer. The presence of the Holy Spirit was so powerful there that we were immediately drawn to the gospel message. We could feel the Lord lead us every time we went inside and we weren't the only ones. We were able to see how the Lord brought the lost to Himself and were able to see how He and His church loved those that the world had rejected.

Jordan and I were moved at practically every service we attended. As new believers, we simply ate it all up. Brother Jimmy seemed to speak exactly what the Holy Spirit led him to speak and it was this kind of submission to the Spirit that helped those messages to impact our hearts on a spiritual level, not just an emotional one. His sermons were powerful and touched so many that came to listen.

Throughout our salvation experience and our joining of the church, I continued to be extremely concerned that people might find out how much of a mess our lives really were. I was anxious around the people before the service started and would even avoid eye contact with others because I was afraid they might kick me out if they discovered everything we were going through at the time.

I even thought someone had come to know some of our secrets because Brother Jimmy seemed to talk about the things we struggled with during his sermons, but he never came to talk to us about them, and he never asked us to leave the church, so I was more than a little confused. I guessed that God was leading him to talk about the things I needed to hear.

Brother Jimmy addressed our situation and problems with almost every sermon he spoke and I was growing and healing with every word he said. He was able to give me the reassurance, hope, or answer that I was looking for. Whether the answer was to pray or take some specific action, God used Brother Jimmy to make it clear to me that there was a way out of the mess I was in.

Sometimes the answer was as simple as letting go of something that I had been hanging on to - letting go of resentments or some irrational hope that I had for life. He always seemed to have the answer.

That's when I realized that God really did use Brother Jimmy during the sermon. It was more than a way to get people to join the church and it was more than a way to get people to stop doing things they knew they needed to stop doing. There was something supernatural to the way he spoke and when he delivered a sermon; there was more in the room than just words.

We still only went for the one-hour service on Sunday mornings in 2011. To be honest, I didn't know that I could take much more. I was learning so much and I was working hard to implement what I was hearing during those sermons alone.

Also, I guess I was a little scared that if I went more often, I'd just find out that these people were just as messed up as the rest of the world and I wouldn't want to go anymore. So we kept going to our Sunday Morning Service and tried to be happy with only that.

We rarely missed a Sunday, and with that, we rarely missed the opportunity to hear from the Lord. The more I was there to listen, the more I kept hearing God encourage me to fully invest myself into this church. God kept telling me that we needed to go for Sunday School and Wednesday Night Service.

Of course, I tried to ignore Him. I tried to convince myself that it wasn't really the Lord or that I just didn't have time. I tried to believe the lie that there was nothing more for me to learn about God or the church, and that if I went to the other services, these people would get to know me and they might not let us stay. Funny how Satan begins to tell you that you are unworthy of God's message and God's church when you really get serious about being a part of them.

I eventually gave in to the Lord's direction and decided to attend Sunday School. Making the decision to go to Sunday School and actually getting settled into a class were two different things. As I said before, the church was very small. In fact, other than children's classes, there were only three options for adults to attend. There was the old men's class, the old women's class, and Brother Jimmy's class.

Brother Jimmy worked hard to grow the discipleship program at our church, but as classes were built from the ground up, few classes were able to survive. Some teachers moved away, and classes dropped off from a lack of teaching.

We really didn't know that we were witnessing the growth of a church. We struggled to find a class that spoke to us where we were. We tried several classes and enjoyed the company, but struggled to know how to keep up in a class where it seemed like every person attending knew more of the Bible than I did. I was so afraid that people would find out how little I knew about what it meant to follow Jesus.

Along the way, Lynn and Connie Jackson started a Sunday school class. These people displayed the love of Christ with everything they did. I could see that God was directing their lives and I wanted to learn how this happened. I loved this couple and knew that they could be a great place to learn, but that didn't seem to calm my anxiety about going to yet another class. Jordan had already started going to the old men's class. That class suited his calm demeanor. Jordan was quiet and contemplative and if an older men's class is anything, it's quiet and contemplative.

In addition to the fact that these older men had the same kind of temperament that Jordan had, they really enjoyed having a young man to minister to. They took Jordan by the hand (metaphorically) and began to teach him what it meant to be a husband, father, and follower of Jesus Christ. They discipled Jordan with a gentle kind of love that completely complemented Jordan's personality and learning style.

Not knowing where to go to class, I just hung out in the nursery until the primary church service started. I felt like I was hiding because I didn't know where to go. I regretted not getting into a class, but my fear kept me from investing myself into any class. I wanted to fit in and wanted people to think I was as developed as they were, or at least, not fully realize how little I knew. I felt ashamed at times that I was at church during Sunday School, but didn't go to class; I just didn't know how to start.

When I heard about Lynn and Connie's class, I finally decided to just take a deep breath, and show up to class by myself. We all started out talking about what we wanted out of this class, like lessons, and so on.

I was the youngest and the newest believer and I didn't know anything. They suggested we should start at the beginning for me, but that didn't even seem to be enough. I went three or four times and decided it wasn't for me. I just couldn't keep up with the lesson.

They flipped back and forth through the Bible looking at so many scriptures that I couldn't keep up. I couldn't even find the right book and chapter fast enough. I really wanted them to tell me the page number, but apparently Bibles don't have the same page numbers. Who knew?

I was still unsure of how to find a verse in the Bible. So, I fell behind and continued to get lost. I wasn't learning anything other than how embarrassing it was that I couldn't keep up and felt like I was holding them back.

The group was completely supportive; it's just that every time we went to a new scripture, everyone waited on me. They would tell me it was okay, but the fact that they had to tell me that made things worse. It was at this low point when I began to experience real spiritual warfare about my discipleship.

I didn't feel like I belonged in Lynn and Connie's class, so I switched to Brother Jimmy's class. I thought that since I learned so much during his sermons, and I didn't understand what was being taught in the other

Sunday School class that it was best that I come to Brother Jimmy's class.

I began to really enjoy Brother Jimmy's Sunday School class and felt like I was starting to learn more in-depth of what the scripture meant. I had heard so many things in our main worship service through the sermons Brother Jimmy would preach, that I began to have many questions. Being in the weekly small group class gave me the opportunity to ask questions and to hear the wisdom that the Lord had given to these believers

One Saturday night, I had a horrible dream about going to Sunday School that next morning. In my dream I was walking down the hallway of the church. I it was scary and dark. It was like a scene from a hospital horror movie.

Every other ceiling light was on and each dark shadow seemed to mask some other kind of evil. Some of the lights were even blinking and hanging off the ceiling by their wires. When I got to the door of Lynn and Connie's class, I peeked my head in to see in the room. There were a few people there, but I developed the distinct feeling that, "I'm not supposed to go there." So I quickly snuck past, avoiding eye contact with the people that were already in the room.

I made my way through the darkened hallway to Brother Jimmy's class. As I approached the door, there was a very scary face on it. There was a black sinking hole in the middle of the door with a ghostly looking face screaming in pain, as if it was being sucked in to this black hole of terror. The cries of help were so loud that I couldn't shut them out. I could feel tears falling down my face, but I couldn't make a sound. I turned and I ran out of church and I didn't look back.

I woke up that morning sweating and filled with fear. I was so scared that I had made the wrong choice about Sunday School.

"What did that dream mean?" I thought.

"Maybe I'm not supposed to be in Sunday School at all."

When we got to church that morning, I could feel my anxiety rising. I was scared and wanted to tell Jordan, but because he had begun to really enjoy the old men's class, I didn't want him to feel like he needed to leave that class just because of a dream I had. He enjoyed it in there and was learning, so I felt bad to ask him to leave, just to be stranded with me.

As in my dream, I walked down the hallway. I could feel the hallway get darker and fear seemed to grow in my heart with every step. At the first door, I peeked in. That same feeling came to my gut that was in my dream; "I'm not supposed to be in this room."

This was getting too weird and the similarities between my dream and reality made that morning that much more intense.

I snuck by the open door, trying desperately to remain inconspicuous, and made my way down the hallway. As I walked to Brother Jimmy's class, I could feel my fear building even more. I was so nervous, scared, and anxious about what would find me when I got to the door that I almost didn't want to go at all.

I know it sounds silly, but I wondered, "Would that face be on the door? Should I just keep walking?" This all felt way too close to my dream!

As I reached the door, a man named Lane Jackson stood in front of it, holding it open. I looked up at him and waited for his face to turn into the sinking black hole from my dream. I tried to make eye contact and act like I wasn't having a nervous breakdown.

Right before I turned to do my best Olympic sprinter impersonation, he smiled and said, "You're coming in here, right? We are glad to have you".

I smiled and went to sit down. I struggled to get to my seat without hyperventilating and as I sat down, my nerves began to return to normal.

God knew that Satan put fear in my heart so that I would not come to Sunday School. He made sure His people were available to help me along the way. A feeling of relief and victory set in and I began to realize that my fear could be overcome with the Holy Spirit's power working through the people of His church.

God came to my rescue to assure me that I was safe in His church and in this class. That day, I knew who Satan was and how he liked to deceive me. I was able to see his lie for what it was. I also got to see, first-hand, how powerful my God is and how seriously He takes the development of His children.

I wanted to fully learn to trust in God so that Satan could never fool me again. Satan must have known that I would fall in love with Sunday School because that's exactly what happened. From that point on, my fear of Sunday School diminished greatly. I was able to go without fear and I was able to learn without shame. I began to develop real relationships with the people in my class and was able to get to know how God was working in the lives of so many people, not just me.

With one victory down, there was another to tackle. I had learned how powerful my God was and had begun to understand the value of obeying God's call on my life, but had not devoted myself to the Wednesday Night service.

I was sure that God had called me to be a part of our whole church, and that included the Wednesday night activities, but I could make a lot of excuses on why I couldn't make it to that service.

"It's too hard to cook dinner and get to church then get home and get everyone ready for bed."

"I like my down time and that's something that I don't want to give up."

"I'm too busy and that would only make me more busy."

Well, God won that battle too and I started going on Wednesday nights. Honestly, Wednesday nights became my favorite Bible time. Brother Jimmy was in teacher mode instead of preacher-mode and that helped me to gather more on each passage that was being taught. Teacher-mode explained more, which I needed, and I got to hear questions being asked by others that helped me to learn even more.

In fact, the church even started serving dinner on Wednesday nights. Now, I had absolutely no excuse to stay home. I didn't have to cook, or clean up, and I got to feast on the Word of God too. What could be better?

Plus, I sent my kids to class and nursery, so I had grown-up time. If you're a stay-at-home mom, grown-up time is hard to come by and can be more valuable than gold. Now that I was committed to the mid-week service, I got to have grown-up time every Wednesday night, being surrounded by God's love.

God was fully aware of my need for this service, even though I wasn't aware of it. I was able to be restored in my spirit, body, and mind. He was able to lead me to the very spot I needed to go so that His people and His Spirit could encourage me. However, I had to follow Him down that path to know that He was waiting for me in the end.

My kids loved Wednesday nights, too. They got to sit with their friends and run around before Bible study. By the time Cotton came into our lives, Jordan and I had been walking in our faith for about nine months. Colt and Cason already had learned to love being at the church. Soon, Colt and Cotton were running down the halls of church and in the sanctuary in between the pews. They felt at home in our church. It was as natural for them to be there as it was to be in our own living room. We all fell in love with the joy and acceptance we received from our church.

Eventually, I became a part of every church event I could be. Sunday School, Sunday Service, Wednesday Night Service, Nursery Committee, Prayer Committee, Music, events the church hosted, etc. It got to the point that I was at the church two to four times a week. The boys would get so excited when they found out we were going to church, even if it was for a committee meeting. I didn't do these things because I felt like I had to. I did them because I loved being there. I loved the people and I loved what the Lord was doing in and through my life as a result of being a part of this wonderful group.

One of the most effective programs in our church was a group called Apples of Gold. This was a ministry for women and it was a program that allowed older women to invest into the younger women of the church. It was an amazing time that God used to change my heart toward my husband.

We had grown closer together ever since we gave our hearts and lives to the Lord and our commitment to church helped us to know how to do that more, but my dominating and independent attitude prevented us from being able to experience all that God had for us as a couple. We continued to struggle to be a couple and even though we were more in love than ever before, there was something holding us back.

Honestly, if I had not already been growing in my walk with the Lord and had I not already seen how loving my church family really was, I don't know that I could have listened to these lessons with an open mind. They suggested that I should submit to the authority of my husband and allow him to lead our family. It didn't mean I was going to be less important than I had been previously. I would simply be asserting myself in the role that God designed for me to fill.

I learned what a Godly wife could be. I took a long, hard look at myself and found that I didn't like the woman I saw. I was not who God wanted me to be. No wonder things seemed to be broken at home. I reflected on the idea that to be a wife was to play a very specific role in the home. I was able to see that by attempting to be the father and mother to my children, I was resisting God's blessing for both Jordan and myself. I wanted things to work, like they had never worked before, so the lessons became relevant to me. I began to wonder how I could make a real difference in my family.

I opened my heart to what the Lord had to say, even if it meant that I had to change who I had been for my family. I knew He would give me the strength and wisdom to do it.

I can still remember what I was thinking at the first meeting.

"Submission? To who? Why should I bow down to this man?"

I was taught to never depend on a man for anything. I even thought deep down that I didn't need one. He was lucky to have me. I was so wrong that it felt like a slap in the face. And the craziest part of it all was that I couldn't argue with any of the things that were being said because it came straight out of the Bible! However, not having a leg to stand on had never stopped me from questioning things in the past, so I jumped right into the mix with my issues.

My first question was, why do I have to start doing everything for him while he just works and comes home? The lingering thought of the Biblical foundation of all this information kept eating at my heart. Not to mention, how much I respected all the women that were leading this group. I knew that I wanted what they had with their husbands and I knew that I needed to make some changes, but I was so unsure about turning my back on everything I knew. But, I gave it a try anyway.

The first night I cooked was a real shocker for Jordan. He came in the house and found food ready and I could immediately see the wheels turning in his mind, trying to figure out what was coming next. His eyes darted around the house, wondering if he had missed something or if he had forgotten a birthday or anniversary, or if I had burned down some part of the house and tried to cover it up with the smell of partially burned chicken fried steak.

I tried to casually let him know that I had decided to make cooking part of my routine. Though it was supposed to be a passing thought in an otherwise mundane conversation, the statement seemed to permeate the topic to the point that Jordan choked a little on his meal and had to take a drink to regain his composure. He cleared his throat and chuckled a little, still not sure of what all was going on.

Later he told me that he thought it might last two weeks, if he was lucky, but the weeks turned in to months. The new element in our routine became commonplace and he became less and less surprised at the sight of me in the kitchen or food on the table. That surprise turned into gratitude on his part. He became grateful for what I was doing for him, and gracious toward me in so many other ways.

Another topic in Apples of Gold was that we should set the tone for the conversation we hoped to have in the first five minutes of our encounters with our husbands. I wanted our conversations to be more positive and more productive so I started making sure that when he got to the house, I not only had a plate of food and cold glass of milk waiting for him, I also had a focus for our conversation.

So, as I set his plate down in front of him, I would start our conversation with, "How was your day, Honey?"

That one question was magic. It didn't seem to matter how hard his day was or how serious a problem was when I started our time with those words, I told him I loved him with the way I served him. I told him he mattered by asking about his day and I let him know that his words had value by letting him talk.

The longer I cooked and the better our communication became, the better I understood what the Bible meant when it told me as a wife to submit to Jordan as my husband. It wasn't that Jordan was my king and I was his servant. It was that he was my Adam and I was his Eve. He was my leader and I was his helpmate. And it worked; it really worked.

When a decision came up, normally I would have handled it for both of us without even involving Jordan, but this time, I told Jordan. I explained the situation to him and told him my opinion and asked him how he would handle it.

After he wiped the shocked look of his face, he told me what he thought. I could see him bracing himself for some kind of rebuttal from me, but when it never came, he began to relax. I told him that I would support the decision he made and if there was a way that I could help him, I would be willing to do that, but I trusted him to take care of things.

By this point, Jordan was looking around the room for hidden cameras. He didn't really know what to do at this point because I had never butted out of a decision like this, but the next day, things were done and the issue was in the past.

The more I let him lead, the easier it was to support him. Our relationship had never been this strong because the relationship had never been what God wanted.

I could finally see those lessons from Apples of Gold paying off. We didn't fight as much, mainly because I gave him a few minutes to tell me what he thought. Then after giving my opinion, I trusted him to have the final say. It was hard when he didn't do what I suggested, but somehow it worked out.

Soon we started talking about everything. We discussed work decisions, and children decisions together, and I allowed him to take the lead. I also learned that the more I supported Jordan by cleaning, cooking, taking care of our children, being a secretary, wife, and spiritual helper, the closer we became, which in turn resulted in more openness.

I enjoyed seeing his face every morning when he had a hot meal waiting for him and Cason was ready for school. When he came home and saw his house clean and dinner on the table, we were free to engage one another without the issues of everyday life hanging over our head. He worked hard for his family and it pleased me and God. I did my job in the home, and it pleases him and God, so we were blessed by it.

I had to learn that God would take care of me.

Being submissive to God taught me to be submissive to Jordan. I learned to have the faith to know that God's Word was best and I would be blessed for following it.

Now, looking back, being submissive to God and Jordan has been the biggest blessing. I was free of the regret of making the wrong decisions for our family. I no longer felt guilty for trying to parent my husband. I didn't feel powerless or less strong at any point in the process. I felt equal. The difference was, by partnering with Jordan in our home, I was a part of something better than it ever was before. I felt like I had a purpose and was empowered to take it on.

The church that we stumbled upon was the perfect place for us. It became our second home. We all felt safe to be who we were. There was no judgment at our church, only God's love. People at our church didn't care if I had holes in my clothes, or messy hair. Even Brother Jimmy just hugged us and said he was so happy we came. The people who came to church became my new best friends and family.

I understood what it felt like to be a part of a church family, to be a part of a love and cause much greater than myself, and I wanted more. Every chance I got to read and learn or do something for God, I did. Still, to this day, I have that passion of wanting more of what God has to offer. I want more of what God offers because He has been so faithful to give me perfect gifts. I have trusted Him with my life and He has provided me with gifts that only He can give. He offered me real love and showed me what that love looked like through the people of His church.

I really needed that kind of love and I needed to know that this was a place where I could spend the rest of my life, because the events that were to come would place me in an even greater need. I would need a family to lean on and a God to hold me up. Without my new relationship with Jesus and His church, the next few months would have been impossible to endure.

A Tragic Sight

$\mathcal{I}$t was the end of May in 2013 and Cason was finally out of school, so he was immediately bored out of his mind. He didn't have to be home more than a few days before he longed for stuff to do. Colt and Cotton weren't old enough for school yet, so they didn't know that anything was different, other than their big brother got to stay home with them. They loved their big brother, and as a result, they loved the summer. Being that Jordan worked on irrigation wells, the summer was his busy time at work.

I loved having Cason, Colt, and Cotton home at the same time and tried to set up fun play dates so that our time wasn't spent sleeping in and watching too much TV. We wanted to enjoy our time together and do as many things as we could, so we planned day trips to go to the park, or even go to a water park. In our rural neighborhood, kids know each other so well that they love to go to a friend's house, or go get a friend or two and eat at Chick-fil-A. Really, they liked to play on the big slides and stuff, but they told me they were hungry just so they could play there. They had so much fun wherever they were.

One of our favorite things to do during the summer was stay home and just spend the day outside playing on the club house with swings, riding bikes down the driveway, or jumping on the trampoline with the water sprinkler.

Summers in West Texas are incredibly hot and the thought of having to endure yet another one without some kind of help was almost too much. So when the summer of 2013 was approaching, I told Jordan we were buying a pool so the kids and I could keep cool during the summer months. In the past, we had attempted to beat the heat with some smaller investments like kiddie pools, or a Slip-n-Slide, but since Cason was more than four feet tall and the boys had grown to really love water, I thought it would be fun for the whole family to get to play. Kiddie pools can get a little cramped with three active boys and their overheated mom. I researched pools for about a month and found the best deal on a big above-ground pool. The kids were so excited, and to be really honest, so were Jordan and I.

The pool finally came in and we started getting it set up. The blue liner was held together with white poles and the whole time we were setting it up, the kids jumped around as excited as they could be. We put it up in our front yard, like the rednecks we are, and wasted no time filling it up and jumping in. In all reality, we put it in the front yard because that was the only spot that was flat and big enough for the giant pool. When we got it set up, we immediately started to fill it. All three boys got in to play while the water was low, but since the water came from a well, it was FREEZING! So, they didn't stay long.

It took about two weeks to get warm enough for me to get in, but the kids would brave the cold for a few additional minutes each day. The only thing worse than the heat during the summer is the blowing dust. It was hard to keep the cover on the pool and the dirt out. It was a chore to keep the pool ready for the kids, but it was so much fun to play in, I really didn't mind.

During our weekly visit to Walmart for groceries, we made sure we walked through the pool section to ensure we were current on all our pool toys. It wasn't always the kids who found the best toys; sometimes I'd surprise them all with a unique snag of my own. That pool was fun, even when we weren't in it. We had toys that would sink so Cason could go get them and others that floated for Colt and Cotton. We found a swim vest/suit for Cotton and some good arm floaties for Colt.

The first few times in the pool, I had Colt on one arm and Cotton on the other. After a minute, I would hold Colt with just my hand to show him he could swim and not sink because of the arm floaties. Soon he took off swimming like a fish. Cotton, on the other hand, wouldn't let me go. He liked to splash, but didn't want any part of swimming by himself. When he finally did let go a few times, the swim vest/suit made him roll over to his back in the water. When I would try to let him go, he'd start to rock back and get so scared. I tried to show him that he was safe that way, but he hated it, so the next time I was in the store, I decided to try arm floaties to see if that would make a difference.

When we got back to the pool with the arm floaties rather than the life vest, Cotton let me hold his hand, but he still wasn't sure about letting me go. Cason and Colt really tried to help. "Look Cotton. Like this. See, we're floating."

I decided to take his attention off the security of my hand by turning it into a game. I gave him one of the million floating toys we had and told him to throw it into the pool. He threw it in as hard as he could and Cason or Colt would swim to get it. Then, they would throw it back and I'd help Cotton get it. At first, I'd just grab the toy if it was too far away and hand it to him, but after a while, I'd let him reach for it. With every throw, he got that much stronger and that much more sure of his ability to float. So when the moment came that he reached out for the toy and finally let go of my hand, I just cheered him on. "Kick, kick, kick!" I yelled.

He cried for a few seconds, but when his brothers

joined in the celebration, he started to believe that he could do it after all.

"Look, you're swimming!! Get the toy, Cotton! YAY! You're swimming." They cheered, and that was all it took; Cotton was a fish too. Not five minutes later, he was climbing on the ladder and jumping off into the pool just like his brothers.

I had rules governing how the pool would be used. The ladder will always be out of the pool until we are using it. Mom was the only one who could put the ladder in the pool. Once everyone had gotten out of the pool, the ladder must be removed immediately. The younger boys must always have their floaties on while the ladder is in the pool. No one is to be around the pool without an adult. We were determined to be the safest pool owners on the planet and the kids and I had several conversations about pool safety even before the pool arrived. "That way," I thought, "We will know exactly how to act around the pool. "

That summer, the sun burned brighter and hotter than ever. It was like the sun's rays beat down on us more, just because we had the pool to comfort us. The pool was great and now that all the boys were swimming, they didn't want to go out to eat with friends as much. They wanted all their friends to come see us and play in the pool.

We had my best friend, Lydia, and her three kids over to play more times than I can even count. Her oldest was Seth. He and Cason were the same age and both attended the same elementary school. Next was Emma, who was five. She and Colt like to play together, and the slight age difference didn't seem to faze him at all. Last, but never least, was Chloe. She was three years old and loved Cotton. Any time Lydia and her children came to play, the kids would pair up and the rest of the day seemed like it flew by. Sometimes, Lydia and I would play with them, but other times, we'd just sit in the shade and watch our kids play their hearts out.

Maybe it was because Colt and Cotton were so close in age or maybe because they looked so similar, but sometimes Colt and Cotton would switch friends for a day. Emma didn't seem to mind all that much. She loved to "mother" Cotton. One day, I was babysitting all the kids and they were playing in the mud (because that's how we roll). When it was time to get cleaned up, all I had to do was tell the kids that play time was over and Emma took charge and got all four of them in the tub. She washed all the other kids and dried them. It was so cute!

For Cotton's second birthday, of course, we had a pool party! We had his party a day early so we could have it on Saturday and we tried to utilize our pool as much as we could. Our plan was to let loose of our senses. We had lots of water balloons, water guns, and splashing in the pool, so we got started getting all our supplies ready for the big day. I knew it was going to take me a whole day to fill up all those water balloons, so Cotton figured out a way to help while Colt took a nap. After I would get one filled and tied, he would carry it over to the wagon. He would place it gently in the wagon and would get so excited that he would jump up and down for a job well done. Then, he would come running back over to me with his fat kid run and a cheesy grin on his face to get more balloons.

He especially loved it when a balloon had a hole in it. He would stick out his tongue and try to drink the water and when the tiny stream of water hit him in the eye or nose, he would kick his knees up and giggle. We just sat there and filled balloons for hours. He loved every minute of it. When we were done, we had a kiddie pool full of water balloons ready for the party.

There were about ten or more kids who came to the party, and several parents as well. After eating cake and opening presents, the adults couldn't help themselves and had to join in. It started with one parent getting shot by a water gun or being hit by an errant balloon. It was like the shot heard round the world. Soon, it was the kids against Jordan and Lydia's husband, Cody. Cotton and I filled up about 200 water balloons that lasted maybe five minutes. Soon, some of the moms got involved. They picked up the water guns and started to join in with the kids on the relentless assault of the dads.

In an effort to stay dry, I sat next to the great grandparents. I falsely assumed that being close to them would result in my being left alone, but in my family, that doesn't work. Soon, I was soaking wet and had no way to get back at anyone because I hadn't grabbed a gun when I had the chance. Because of my proximity to the grandparents, they were all soaked as well. I kind of felt bad for putting them in the line of fire, but they ended up having a blast too. I'm not sure who had the most fun, the kids or the adults.

On July 12, 2013, Lydia's three kids came back over to swim and play with the boys. While Jordan and I were sitting outside watching the older four kids play in the pool, Cotton just ran around playing with toys on the concrete. It was odd that he didn't want to be in the pool with the other kids, but Cotton loved playing with his tractors. He would push them around and make believe he was a big time farmer. He would come running up to us, say something silly, then would run off laughing like it was the funniest thing ever. He was just in his own world that day.

Then, out of nowhere I hear, "Ooh no, that's gross!" I jumped up to see what had happened and found that Colt had swallowed too much water and threw up in the pool. I didn't want the kids to swim in the pool like that, so I got everyone out of the pool, wrapped them in towels, and sent them inside. I went to the garage to get the chemicals to clean the pool. I put the chemicals in the pool and went inside to help the kids get into dry clothes.

My friend's kids wanted to stay the night, so I had them call their mother to ask. After they talked to their mom, I got on the phone to tell her it was fine, I'd love for them to stay if she could come drop off an overnight bag. When I hung up, I realized that I hadn't heard Cotton's voice with the other kids. I went walking around the house looking for him, but I couldn't find him. I walked across the house to the playroom where most of the kids were and he wasn't there. I went back to the sunroom where Jordan was and told him that I couldn't find Cotton. I glanced out the windows to the back yard, but didn't see him, so I went toward the front door.

I peeked through one of the front windows that looked out onto the patio to see if Cotton was playing out there and I suddenly realized that the gate that separated the enclosed patio to the pool was open. I immediately realized what might have happened.

I started saying, "No… No… No…"

As I ran out the door toward the pool, I saw the ladder still in the pool. The ladder wasn't supposed to be there. It wasn't supposed to be in the pool when we weren't outside to watch. How did it get there? Did I leave it there? Thoughts raced through my head in the few short steps it took to get to the pool.

As I ran, I started screaming, "NO! NO! NO! NO!"

When I got to the pool, there was Cotton floating. I didn't try to climb in; I just jumped in and grabbed him. As I lifted him out of the water, I saw Jordan running over to the pool. He heard me screaming and came running outside and was standing beside the pool by the time I got to Cotton. I threw him to Jordan and jumped out of the pool running inside to grab my phone to dial 9-1-1. I couldn't feel my heart beating.

All I could do was think, "I had to save him. This can't happen to me. Focus! I have to save him."

Since I was soaking wet, I was having a hard time dialing the number on my touch screen cell phone. Seconds seemed like an eternity as I tried to get the number punched into the phone. Running back outside, Jordan had Cotton laying on the ground doing CPR. I told Jordan to be careful not to break his ribs.

All I remember was thinking, "This isn't real! No, Cotton can't leave me. I worked so hard to have him. This can't be happening!"

I don't even remember the phone ringing, but suddenly the 9-1-1 operator answered. I tried to answer her questions without yelling, but I was in such shock that she couldn't understand me.

I just kept repeating my address and saying, "I need an ambulance, hurry please, just hurry".

Jordan grabbed the phone and walked off to talk to the operator. I gave mouth-to-mouth to Cotton. He threw up.

"YES!!" I thought. "That's right, get that water out and come back to me."

Jordan pushed on his chest some more. I kept saying, "Cotton, come back to me. You can't leave me. Just breathe, baby, just breathe."

The CPR wasn't working. Jordan walked off, on the phone again, and I grabbed Cotton in my arms. I started rubbing his head and face as I rocked him. He had already lost all the purple/blue color he had in his lips. He was so pale and lifeless.

I started yelling, "You can't leave me! You can't! I'm so sorry I wasn't there. I should have been there! You can't leave me! You can't leave me!"

Jordan came back and tried to take Cotton.

I yelled at him, "Don't take him from me, you can't take him from me".

He walked off on the phone again. When he came back he asked, "What do we do?"

I looked at him and said, "Call Brother Jimmy."

I looked back at Cotton and I told him, "You left me, didn't you? I'm so sorry I wasn't there. You weren't supposed to leave me. Oh, Cotton, why did you leave me? Come back!"

When I looked up again I saw the kids standing around me in shock. I hollered at them to go back inside.

Jordan came back and said, "We have to do more CPR."

We had only stopped a minute or two ago, so we laid him down and started pumping his chest again. Still, Cotton just laid there pale and lifeless.

A state trooper pulled up, jumped out of his car, and ran up to us. He started to ask a few questions. I tried my best to answer them, but it was so hard to stay focused.

I asked him, "What do we do?"

He said, "Y'all are doing more than most do." He was trying to be reassuring, but his words seemed so hollow and they echoed in my ears.

"Keep doing CPR; I hear the ambulance. It will be here soon!" He yelled.

Lydia pulled up and jumped out and started panicking. "What do you want me to do?" She asked frantically.

"Go stay with the kids!" I shouted. "They keep coming out here and I don't want them to see this".

I held Cotton's hand as I watched Jordan do CPR. I pleaded again, "Cotton, please don't leave me. Please, I need you. I'm so sorry. Please come back to me."

Lydia came back outside just in time to move her car as the ambulance pulled up. I reluctantly sat back a little to let them get to work. They asked even more questions. I tried to answer, but I was still in such shock of what was really happening that I don't even know what I was saying. I felt so helpless. I felt like I should have been able to help him. I felt like I should have prevented this. What was I going to do?

When I looked up again, I saw Brother Jimmy. I didn't know what to feel. My thoughts, words, and feelings kept getting jumbled up inside me. Before I could say anything, Brother Jimmy laid his hand on us and started to pray. I didn't really hear what he was praying because I was continuing to plead with little Cotton to come back to me. Then, I began to feel an overwhelming sense of hope – a sense that, with this entire scene going on, I wasn't alone.

I watched the machines that the paramedics were using and I begged God for a heartbeat. Cotton's lips started to get blue and purple colors back to them and then I heard one of the paramedics yell, "I got a faint one!"

Oh, my heart stopped! "Please, Cotton, come back! Just come back. God, this is your time. Please give me back my baby!"

I could feel arms around me. People of the community were there and some of my family had gotten there by that time. I had been so focused on Cotton that I didn't see all the cars and people show up. I was so grateful for their love, but I couldn't take my eyes off Cotton. I was so afraid that if I looked away he would be gone and I was hoping for a glance. Just a twinkle in his eye that would let me know that everything was going to be ok. I wanted a twitch in his cheek or a gasp of air that would help me know that my sweet Cotton wasn't lost.

A paramedic broke the chaos and told the state trooper to go shut down the highway so the helicopter could land.

Then, the paramedic looked at me and said, "Ma'am we are going to take him to University Medical Center."

I said, "Okay, just save him, please, just save him."

I gave Cotton one last look and pleaded again, "Please, baby boy, come back to me. I'm so sorry. I will be right there; don't give up yet. Keep fighting; keep breathing."

I got up and ran inside to put on dry clothes. In a matter of seconds, I was dressed, grabbed my purse, and jumped into Jordan's truck. I looked in the mirror to see the helicopter still in the highway. Jordan drove through the field, past the trooper's barricade, then crossed the median on the divided highway to get on to the north-bound lane.

Jordan started to pray, "Lord, please let my little boy be alive when we get to the hospital". I looked up in time to see the helicopter fly over. I started pleading "Cotton, I'll be right there. Hang on, baby."

I knew this would be the only time I would have to call anyone. So, I grabbed my phone and called my mom. She and my father had gone out of town for a golf tournament.

My mom answered the phone, "Hey Baby."

I took a second to try to clear my throat from crying and said the words for the first time, "Momma, Cotton just drowned in our pool."

My mom said, "What, Honey? I can't understand you."

I cleared my throat again and said it even louder and as clearly as I could, "Cotton just drowned in our pool. We are on our way to the hospital now. I will try to keep you updated."

My mom immediately told my dad why they had to come home. She said "Baby, we will be right there. Love you."

After I hung up, I helped Jordan watch the road as we drove through red lights and dodged traffic. Neither of us spoke.

As we pulled up to the hospital, we could see that the helicopter made it and could only hope that it arrived in time. It was so hard to let my baby ride here without me, but I knew they would beat us there. Our cousin was already there, so we jumped out and let him park our truck. We ran inside and told them our son was just flown in on the helicopter. The staff led us to the back where we had to sit in a waiting room. Waiting again. How were we going to wait in this room when our boy was so close?

The nurse said, "The doctor will come in shortly."

Jordan prayed again, "Lord, please let my boy live."

The door opened; my heart stopped. I whipped my head toward the door and saw Brother Jimmy. My heart started beating again. He sat down and prayed with us again.

A minute later, the door opened, and again my

heart stopped. I couldn't breathe when I saw that it was a doctor. What did she know? Where was my Cotton? Would he be ok?

"Ma'am, I'm sorry. After someone hasn't been breathing for more than seven minutes, there isn't a good chance of them making it."

I was stunned. "He didn't make it?" I begged.

She shook her head and said, "No, I'm so sorry. We tried."

I could feel the tears slide across my face and fall to the floor while I said, "I know you did. Thank you so much. Can I see him?"

She said, "Yes ma'am. Let us get it cleaned up back there and someone will come get you."

As she left, we cried. I had never imagined such pain. I had never thought my heart could feel this way. It felt like my heart was being stabbed over and over and left to bleed. I thought, "My baby boy is really gone."

I prayed the only thing that came to my lips: "Oh, God, be with me, I need you. Give me the strength to go through this. Hold my Cotton tight. I'm holding You to Your word that I will see him again."

The nurse came into the waiting room where we sat and waited. Jordan, Brother Jimmy, and I walked back to the room where they tried to save Cotton. Tears fell as my heart broke a thousand times over. Seeing him lying there I could feel my nerves beginning to give way. I was scared of what was about to happen to our family, yet at the same time, I was so happy to be there, to hold him again. I lost sight of everything and everyone. Nothing was real to me but my baby and my agony.

The ride to the hospital had been so horrible, not being able to touch or see him. I grabbed his hand and smiled while my tears threatened to fill the room. How peaceful he looked, lying there so still.

Rubbing his head, I said, "My beautiful little boy, I love you so much. I'm so sorry I wasn't there, but you're in a better place. I don't think I can let you go though. You're so beautiful."

I held his hand while friends, family, and church family came in and out. They would hug Jordan and me. Some cried, some touched Cotton, some would pray with us, and some couldn't bear to look at Cotton lying there. I could feel a spark of love from each person that was brave enough to come into that room. I knew I was going to be okay. I got to hold and touch Cotton. I knew his spirit wasn't there, but just holding his hand was enough. I couldn't do anything but thank God for holding me up. Even at a time where I wanted to be mad or angry with God, I couldn't. I knew that He was showing me His love through His body, the church. It wouldn't replace my baby, but it could help me stand for the moment.

Sometime after midnight, some nurses came into the room needing to get it ready again, which meant it was time for us to leave and go home.

"NO," my heart cried. "I can't leave him. I don't want to leave him."

I had to convince myself, "I will touch and see him again soon, but we have to go in case they need this room to save another life. Our other boys need us now."

I gave Cotton one last kiss and told him I loved him. Then, I grabbed my purse and held Jordan's hand as we made our way back through the waiting room.

It was like everything had been frozen in time. All the other patients and families in the main waiting room sat still as they watched us go by. It was as if no one dared to move or say anything. It was as if we were in a movie and they all knew what just happened. We moved so slowly and my heart ached in disbelief that this was really happening. I was really about to walk out of this building without my child, but when we got to the outer door of the hospital, there was a gift from God waiting for us. There were so many people waiting for us.

As I saw all the people waiting to lift us up, all I could think was, "What are all these people doing here? I know it has to be past midnight by now."

I could feel a warmth and hope overwhelm my body. With every hug I got, I felt stronger. It was like they gave me the very strength I asked for, one kind word, and one warm embrace at a time.

Our friends and family asked if they could drive

us home, but Jordan and I wanted to be alone together. After we saw each and every person there, we made our way to our truck. I got a call saying my mom and dad were on their way to the hospital, so we waited for a minute in the parking lot. Most of the people who came started to make their way home. I began to feel the wind, see the lights of the hospital, and hear the everyday sounds of the city. My head felt empty. I didn't know what to say or do. I just knew that I felt empty.

A few minutes later, the silence was broken when I saw my brother pull up to the hospital and walk over to see us. I hadn't seen my brother in such a long time. The feeling of comfort, joy, hurt and love sprang to my heart and I wept again as we hugged. After a minute, I realized he was squeezing me so tight I couldn't breathe. I told him to call mom and tell her to meet us at my house. Jordan and I said one last good-bye to people standing around us. Then we got in the truck and made our way home without our little boy.

Jordan and I talked on the way home. We talked about how we weren't going to let this come between us - how we wanted to walk through this together. He suggested that we make sure to surround ourselves with people who loved us and could support us. We would not pull away from other people. We needed them now more than ever.

God blessed me with an amazing man. If he had not been there to guide me, I would have been lost. On that ride home, there was just the two of us, but God was there with us too. It was like He was the one putting the words in our mouths and propping up our bodies when our human strength failed us. I might have felt empty, but I never felt alone.

When we picked up Cason and Colt from grandma's house, Colt was already asleep. After we got on the road to head home, Cason asked, "Where's Cotton, mommy?"

I said, "Baby, he went to live with Jesus. I'm sorry."

No one really said anything after that. There wasn't much that could be said.

One Day at a Time

When we got home from picking up the boys, my parents and sister were already at our house waiting for us. We just hugged and cried. They didn't really ask any questions. Again, there wasn't really any need for questions when you don't have answers. Everyone was quiet and just sat on the porch and stared past the pool into the black night. After we sat and cried together until late that night, we hugged each other again and they left promising to be back early the next morning.

After we got the kids to bed that night, I told Jordan I couldn't stand to see that pool anymore. Every time I thought about the pool, I thought about my Cotton, and every time I thought about my Cotton, the image of that pool leapt back into my head. I wanted it taken down and thrown in the trash. I really knew that the pool wasn't to blame for all this; I just wanted something to feel like I felt. So Jordan went outside and got a water hose to start draining it.

I couldn't go to sleep that night. The images of that day floated in my mind. They would linger until I swatted them away and then would return like a plague. I couldn't think of anything or see anything in the house that didn't remind me of my baby. Every time I thought that I had pulled myself back together, the images of my boy face down in the water came rushing back. But the events of the past day paled in comparison to the thought that I would never hear my sweet boy laugh again. I would never see him run, or grow, or hear his cute little giggles. I would never know who he would have become. The thought of having to live without my sweet Cotton was unbelievable.

"My little boy is really gone. Never coming back."

At times that night, as I dozed from exhaustion, I would have to convince myself that it was real. I had to retell myself that I had lost one of my sons. I didn't want to think about it in the first place, but I wanted to be the voice of truth even less. But the truth is what I needed. I needed to know that it was real, that all of these things had happened, but I also needed to know that the truth would hold me up. I had experienced Satan's lies in the past and had been beaten down by fear, but I didn't have to do that anymore. I could stand alongside my God and He would win this war for me. All I had to do was get through the night. All I had to do was make it 'til morning. If I could only get some sleep.

Blessed are those who mourn, for they shall be comforted.
Matthew 5:4

Saturday, July 13, 2013

The next morning, I woke up and got in the shower like it was any other day. I tried to start the day as if nothing happened, but that possibility dissolved the instant the water hit my face. I wept as the water washed my tears away. I was unable to control my sorrow. I hadn't really been alone since all this started and I allowed myself to grieve. I knew that the Lord would hold me up. I knew that He would restore my strength.

I prayed, "Lord, I need strength and guidance. I don't understand why a miracle didn't happen, but I know you will take care of Cotton for me. Tell him I'm sorry that I wasn't there in time and that I love him."

As I got ready for the day, I thought, "What am I supposed to do now?"

I wasn't really asking about the coming years, which would be incomprehensibly difficult, but right now. What was I supposed to do right now?

The pool was slowly draining and I tried not to look at it. It was a constant reminder of all that happened the day before. Jordan, on the other hand, stood at the pool, lost in thought. He wasn't really doing anything. He just stood there, half looking at the water, and half staring into oblivion. He gently flicked the water at the pool's edge, but seemed somehow shielded from everything else in the world.

I went to see if he needed anything, not that I could really do anything for him. I couldn't even figure out how I was supposed to deal with all this. I just knew he needed me to be there. He needed his wife, just like I needed my husband.

I asked if I could do anything to help. He shook his head and stared into the pool water as it slowly drained. I paused a moment, trying to come up with something to do to comfort him. I tried to conjure some kind of statement that could help both of us put the previous day in perspective, but nothing came. My mind was blank and the sights and sounds of that morning echoed in my ears and filled my mind to the point that I couldn't stand there next to the pool for another second.

As I went back into the house, I tried to pick up where I left off the day before. I looked for laundry to do, or a floor to vacuum, or dishes to clean, but I had already done it. I only found the muddy clothes from the day before. Brief moments of comfort softened the angst in my heart and soul and then I'd catch a glimpse of Jordan outside, or the edge of the pool out of the corner of my eye, and I'd start to cry at the thought of Cotton floating in it just a few hours ago.

One of our neighbors brought breakfast for us and saw how slowly the pool was draining and how much it was bothering Jordan and me. They quickly left and came back with a big tank and about 5 or 6 other guys to help drain and remove the pool. They got the pool drained and taken down pretty quickly. It got Jordan off the edge of the pool and back to work. He was so used to working with his hands and being able to fix whatever was broken. This was just one thing he wasn't able to fix on his own. I was grateful that the pool was going to be gone sooner, but I was eternally grateful that these men allowed Jordan to be involved. Not that he would have let them work without him, but it was good for him to be a part of something that brought me such relief.

Once I saw the pool folded up and hauled off, I began to feel some of the weight of grief lift off my chest. I wasn't as likely to have that flash of memory because when I looked out my window, all I saw were our pecan trees. I didn't have to be reminded by that blue and white flash anymore.

Our family started to make their way over to our house and we hugged, and loved, and even laughed ourselves into a better state of mind. Tears were still the constant theme most of that morning as I paced around the house. I'm not really sure where I was trying to go or how I was going to get there; I just felt like I needed to be moving. I needed to try to walk away from the pain I felt for the absence in my life, but there was no way I could escape that turmoil. Before that day, I had never lost anyone close to me, so I didn't know what to do. I just kept praying for strength and kept feeling Jesus give me strength with every hug, with every story, with every laugh. He was infusing me with strength, hope, and joy through every visitor that day. I needed them, like I needed Him.

Rejoice with those who rejoice, weep with those who weep.
Live in harmony with one another.
Romans 12:15-16a

When the boys woke up, I hugged them a little tighter than usual and I thanked God for them.

Colt asked, "Mommy, where's Cotton?"

I repeated what I had told Cason the night before. "Honey, he went to live with Jesus last night."

"Mommy, did he go to the bottom of the pool and didn't come up?" Colt asked.

"Yes." I answered, "He got in the pool without his floaties and he couldn't swim."

"Momma, Cotton is going to come back to life and play with me." Colt replied resolutely.

I said, "No, honey, he can't come back. We have to go see him and Jesus one day, but you have to promise me that you won't go see Cotton and Jesus until you are grey headed and have lots of grandkids?"

Colt smiled and ran off to play with Cason. I hurt for Colt. He lost his best friend and wasn't old enough to really understand that Cotton was really gone.

After breakfast, we called Lake Ridge Chapel

funeral home in Lubbock and made an appointment for that day. I didn't really know what we were going to do there and I certainly wasn't ready to answer questions on my own. My parents and Jordan's parents came and even some of our grandparents were there. We needed all the help we could get and Brother Jimmy had worked in family services at a funeral home in the past, so he was a great help to us in those moments. The funeral home personnel were so nice and helpful too.

We started to design our son's funeral all the way down to choices like what kind of casket, where was the service going to be, who would carry the casket, what pictures and songs would be played, and so on. It got to the point that it was very mechanical for me. I was trying to get all the questions right.

Jordan on the other hand, just ducked his head and cried. I could see his heart break at every question and I couldn't do anything to help him. To watch Jordan cry was so hard. He never cried. He didn't even cry this much at his grandfather's funeral. So when he cried, I cried.

When Jordan needed to make a decision about the funeral, he would answer with, "I don't know. I can't believe we have to do this." When he was unable to make a decision, I would try to encourage him.

I whispered to him, "We have to. We have to give Cotton the best we can."

That was my drive to get through that meeting. I

was unable to change what happened to my baby and there was never going to be anything that I could do to overcome the fact that my husband had lost one of his precious sons, but I could do something about how he would be remembered. I could make this funeral a tribute to how much he was loved and how much he loved life.

We had never thought about where we were going to bury our children because nobody ever thinks about that kind of stuff and we didn't even know what cemetery we would use. We had only recently moved to the area where we lived, so we didn't know what do to. Jordan's grandfather had been buried only about ten miles away and his grandmother purchased a couple of extra spots there, so I asked her if we could bury Cotton there. The only stipulation I had was there had to be room for me too. I couldn't leave Cotton there without me. I knew that it would be years before we would be together again, but I wanted to be able to be with him when I was gone.

Jordan's grandmother was happy that we asked and there would be plenty of room for me to. We picked a John Deere green casket with a tractor to go on the inside of the casket. He loved tractors so much, we just thought it would be a great way to honor him. We chose to have the service at our church home in Ropesville and I had to pick songs and pictures and get them back to the funeral home in a couple of days. I had to pick out what clothes I wanted Cotton to wear in the casket. I got my tasks together; I was on a mission. I had a focus and I was determined to make it perfect. I told Jordan the only thing I wanted him to do was to pick who he wanted to carry the casket. He shook his head in agreement.

When we got back home, I immediately started working on pictures and songs. People came over to hug our necks, and brought us food and other items. My cousins and sisters sat with me while we listened to different songs and read different poems. If a song made us cry, we all gathered together and prayed. Never in my life would I have guessed we would hold hands and pray as a family. It just wasn't how we were raised, but it felt so good. It felt good to know that God was able to comfort the people around us. Even though they hadn't lost a son, they had lost Cotton. They lost a nephew, or a cousin, and they had a friend who was hurting. The only real comfort that came to any of us was when we prayed.

I would have to take a break on occasion and go visit with new guests who arrived. I would look around to see my house full of people who loved us. I was able to see how joyous a church could be even when the situation and circumstances were so bleak. No, we didn't all go to the same church, but we all served the same God. We were all being comforted by the Encourager and were being ministered to by each other. I couldn't help but smile. Yet again, God had prepared His people and His church to hold us up. My house was full of laughter, and love, and smiles, and it brought joy to my heart.

There were people in my home that first day after Cotton's death who had been fighting before, but were now standing in the living room laughing together. There were kids playing and running through the house full of joy. I could imagine Cotton sitting in heaven doing the same thing, just sitting and watching everyone around him with a smile.

That afternoon I received a phone call from the sheriff's office. I was terrified as the reality hit that I could be investigated for the death of my son. What if they say I held him underwater? What if they throw me in jail because I left the ladder in the pool?

My mind raced through all the potentially devastating scenarios that could arise, while the sheriff apologized for having to even make the call, and shared his condolences. He told me he would send a deputy to the house the next evening to take more pictures of the pool and to take our official statements. Immediately I realized that I had made Jordan take down the pool too early and I burst in tears of panic.

"I'm so sorry, but I took the pool down." I told the sheriff, "I couldn't bare to look at it another moment when we got home. I'm so sorry. Can I show you where it was or I can see if I have some pictures of it you can use?"

He said "No, ma'am, that is alright. We will use the ones we have. The officer took some pictures the night of the accident, but it was kind of dark, so we wanted new ones."

"Will it be ok if I send my sheriff out tomorrow to get your official statements?"

"Yes, sir, we will be here." I tried to sound steady, even though I wasn't.

He told me he was sorry for my loss again and hung up. I was still worried about it. Could I really be thrown in jail for this? Flashbacks from news reels where parents were sued or jailed because of an accident at their house ran through my head. All I could really do is hold it before my God and let Him take control. There was nothing I could do but trust that God was big enough to handle this too.

As evening approached, people went home. Colt would see a child go home and almost immediately feel the reality of Cotton's absence.

In his loneliness, he would ask me, "Momma, when is Cotton coming back?"

I would tell him, "He's not coming back, honey. He has to live with Jesus 'til we get there."

He had the hardest time with Cotton being gone. Colt didn't like being alone. In all reality, he had never really been alone since Cotton was born. He had always been aware of Cotton's presence and now that he was gone, Colt really didn't know what to do. Colt tried to play like normal, but with the added strain of losing a brother, Cason didn't really want to play. Colt ended up playing alone in his room most of that day. He truly longed for Cotton even though he couldn't find the words to say it. He wanted his best friend there with him.

I remember my mom following me around that night asking me if I ate or what she could do to help after everyone left. I was up cleaning and trying to get the house straight for the next day of visitors. I didn't really speak to her, just shook my head no, but once everyone left, and the silence set in, I missed Cotton. The hurt would come full force. My mom could see me hurting and wanted to take my pain away, but there was nothing that she could do. There was nothing that anyone could do. I was her baby girl and she couldn't stand to see me hurting.

There was no expression on my face. It wasn't that I didn't feel the pain; it was that I had no way to express how much I hurt. All I could really do was the everyday stuff that made me feel normal again, even if it only helped for a moment. Vacuuming, taking the trash out, doing dishes, and switching out laundry were the things that I did before I lost my baby, and the ability to do them now made the pain subside.

My mom followed me everywhere that night trying to get me to talk. I couldn't speak. What am I supposed to say? "Yes I'm hurting, but I can't fix it. This is how it is and I don't want to feel it." Instead, I just went around doing my chores in silence, attempting to numb my pain. Rather than hurting all over again, I just filled my moments with normal so that I could feel that way again.

I didn't think about the loss. I didn't feel the regret of not being there. I didn't care who I hurt in that moment, just as long as I didn't have to feel it. I just didn't want to hurt and being numb was the answer.

Jordan was the only one who could snap me out of it. I'm not sure if it was because he knew what I was going through or knew what to say or that he was just the partner God gave me to walk through this, but I let him in. When Jordan and I finally made it to bed, we talked about how we felt and how the decisions for the funeral were coming. We said how much we missed Cotton's laugh and how empty the house had felt that day, even though there were so many people there. We tried to say how much we loved each other and how important we were to each other. We knew that the majority of people who lose a child like this don't stay together, so we tried to focus on each other as much as we were able. Then, we just held each other and cried until we fell asleep.

Sunday, July 14, 2013

The sun rose on Sunday morning and we got ready for church. It was different in a way because

Cotton wasn't a part of our preparation that day, but there was also a rush of familiarity in an otherwise chaotic experience. We had gotten ready for church so many times before that the morning seemed mundane at times.

But this was no ordinary Sunday, and as much as we tried to make it typical, our experience over the past two days would not let us settle into the routine of church. This day would be a unique kind of Sunday. It would be the first time we went to the church we love without our son. We would celebrate the risen Son of God by sharing our son with Him.

My oldest son, Cason, was going to be baptized that morning after he had surrendered his life to Christ during Vacation Bible School a couple weeks earlier. Brother Jimmy had asked us on Saturday if we still wanted to have the baptism in light of the accident. I asked Cason if he felt like he still wanted to do it. Cason really wanted to be baptized, so we agreed that it would be good for our family to see our faith.

The service that morning was exciting because of the baptism. I tried to focus on Cason that day. I wanted this day to be an amazing memory for him, rather than it being full of sorrow for the loss of Cotton.

Colt cried when I tried to take him to the nursery. He looked scared at the thought of being there without Cotton, so he went with us to the sanctuary. It was good to have him close that day. It was good that he saw his big brother baptized, even if he was too young to really understand how important that day was for all of us.

Since most of the family was already in town, they all came. It was a special day for Cason, as he shared his faith with our church family. We witnessed our son being baptized by Brother Jimmy and felt the joy of our own salvation rekindled in our hearts. We celebrated the fact that one day our own resurrection from the dead would reunite us with our baby boy.

After church, I worked on the songs and pictures for the funeral. I had taken about two thousand pictures of my two-year old, so it took a while. I wanted to make sure that the slideshow for church would be perfect and I poured through the pictures and relived so many great memories of Cotton as he grew.

I also wanted to write something for the service so I worked on that too. I hadn't really written anything like that before, so I worked really hard to make it right. I didn't let anyone read it, except Brother Jimmy. I didn't want anyone telling me I should change this or that. I wanted this to be from me to God and Cotton.

When I took breaks to greet visitors at our house, Cason just seemed to be right there to hug me. Cason was very excited about the baptism and the fact that he had cousins and friends over to play while their parents visited us, but any time I cried that day, Cason was there to try to help. He would hug me again and try to make me laugh. I was blessed to have him next to me. Cason didn't even know how much he helped me that day.

Late in the afternoon, we got a knock on the door. One of our many visitors looked out and saw it was the sheriff. They hollered for me to come to see him and I made my way through the house. I could feel my nerves start to tighten as I greeted him at the door. Since we had a house full, he suggested we go outside to talk. This made me even more nervous. What if he was here to arrest me?

As he spoke, he said he was sorry for my loss and he understands that doing a statement is the last thing I would want to do, but it was procedure. He handed me two pieces of paper and explained how to fill it out. He said that when we were done, we could mail them to the address at the top and if they had any questions they would just give us a call.

One statement was for me and one was for Jordan. I told him thank you again and he left. A sigh of relief fell over me as I realized how Satan tried to use this sweet man to strike fear into my heart. This deputy was only doing his job and did it in a kind and gentle way. There was no reason for fear, because my God had gone before me and had softened the heart of this man so that our encounter could be as painless as possible. I can still remember the genuine sorrow he had in his eyes when he told me how sorry he was for our loss.

That night after everyone left, Jordan and I sat down in different rooms to write our statements.

When we finished I placed them in an envelope ready to go in the mail the next day.

Monday, July 15, 2013

On Monday, Colt had swimming lessons. We had scheduled them a long time ago and discussed whether or not it was the best thing for the time, but decided to go ahead and let Colt go because he needed to have no fear about being in the water. I didn't want my kid's opinion about water to change just because of the accident. They loved playing in water so much that we hoped we could help them love it again.

So, I swallowed my nerves and took him to swimming lessons. I was so glad that Jordan came with me because I held back tears the entire time. Every time I saw Colt go under the water, my heart would start to race and I would try to go save him, but by the time I got to the water, he was fine.

Colt's teacher just looked at me like I was crazy, but I couldn't help it. I was still in such shock about the events of the past Friday that I just couldn't sit still. I had a compulsion to try to help little Colt, but knew it was good for him to experience this with a good teacher. So Jordan had to hold me so I didn't keep jumping up. It was hard to sit there and watch him swim underwater. I would quickly wipe away the tears as they came to my eyes and would try to smile when Colt would look at me so he didn't know I was so fragile. He really was an amazing swimmer. After what seemed like an eternity, Colt was done with swimming lessons. Oh, was I relieved to have him back in my arms, safe and sound.

I had finished the photos and picked out the clothes I wanted Cotton to wear, so we dropped that stuff off at the funeral home while we were in town. Once we got back to the house, I started cleaning again. I did what it took to feel normal again. I tried to find some more solace in the mundane things of my life. It helped having Jordan home with me the whole time. He was such an encouragement to me. I would hear him speak life into me and it just seemed to comfort me in a way that no other words could.

While cleaning, I found two cans of silly string. Jordan and I looked at each other thinking the same thing. We each grabbed one and snuck into the hallway to hide. I hollered for the boys and they came running down the hallway at full speed. We ambushed them and chased them through the house covering them with silly string. It felt good to hear laughter when it was just us again.

After I cleaned up the silly string, we sat down and waited for our family to meet at the house. Jordan and I got the chance to talk to each other again. It was so good to talk to him because he had in incredible sense of wisdom considering the circumstances.

He said, "I feel like God prepared us for this accident in a way."

I said, "Me too! First, He brought us together. Then provided this house for us. Then called us to be at our church and community."

He said, "Yeah, He put us right where we needed to be. He knew this day was coming and that this is what we would need."

At that moment, I realized how grateful I was to be where God wanted me to be. Jordan was right. If we didn't have these wonderful people around us and if they hadn't introduced us to our Lord, how would we have overcome these past few days?

The Funeral I Never Thought I Would Attend

Tuesday, July 16, 2013

    Colt had swimming lessons again the day of the open visitation. Jordan went with me again. It was just as hard as the day before. I flinched and held my breath every time his little head went under the water. I was so uneasy about the fact that Colt was in the water that I could hardly sit still. I even got up and went to the edge of the pool again. Half worried for my Colt and half wrecked from the loss of Cotton, Jordan just held me and tried to tell me it was all going to be okay.

    Soon the teacher dismissed the kids. I wrapped Colt up in a towel and gave him to Jordan. I went to tell the teacher that Colt would be missing lessons tomorrow. I thought if I could get out the reason why then I will tell her, but as I spoke the words I started to cry.

"Colt will be missing tomorrow. He will be here Thursday and Friday though. I hope that is okay?" I asked.

The teacher nodded her head and said, "Yes, that's fine." while looking confused.

I nodded and walked off with the boys.

After we grabbed lunch, we got a phone call from the funeral home saying it was time for us to go see Cotton and make sure everything was ready for visitation that evening. Along the way, I received an email with a link to Cotton's memorial video. I didn't know how I would react to it, so I just waited until we were all in the funeral home parking lot before I watched it.

The funeral home had prepared the video tribute that I had been selecting pictures for, and we were able to watch it. It was beautiful. Those pictures and short videos of Cotton's life brought back such amazing memories and for the briefest of moments, I was able to remember my boy fondly, without my heart bursting with sadness. We watched the video together in the truck before we went into the funeral home. We really just wanted to share that moment with each other and not knowing how we would react, we thought it would be best if we gave ourselves the freedom to grieve in whatever way we needed to before we went inside.

After wiping our tears, we started to get out of the

truck and walk into the funeral home. I really wanted to run in those doors because I knew Cotton was there. It had been about three days since I had seen or touched Cotton. I didn't know what to expect, so my excitement for seeing him was subdued by my anxiety about how he might look. We walked slowly and deliberately to see our little boy.

They opened the doors to the big room and there he was near the front. We slowly walked up to him. The tears flooded my eyes and I started to tremble again. I tuned out everything but the sight of my baby boy in that coffin. I don't know if I was breathing. It was like everything in that giant room faded away and it was just him and me again. When we reached the casket, I froze. I couldn't even move anymore. I saw him for the first time since the hospital and he looked like my little boy again. He was so beautiful.

He wore my favorite outfit, a light-colored plaid shirt with his red hat tilted to the side. He was so peaceful; it was almost like he was just sleeping. I wept as I laid my left hand on his head and my right on his stomach. He was so cold.

I couldn't walk away. I could have stood there forever just so I could touch him. I knew his spirit wasn't there, but I didn't care. I needed to be able to see him. I talked to him and rubbed his head like I always did. Each moment that I got to spend with him in that room were reminders of all the joy we had while Cotton was alive. I just wanted to savor every one of them and remember them forever.

Jordan and the boys came and went, but I couldn't leave. I knew I would be able to see him again in a few hours when the funeral home was open for visitation, but it wasn't the same. I wouldn't get to take him home and feed him dinner and then help him take a bath and get ready for bed. I wasn't going to get to tell him stories and hear his cute little giggles anymore. I would never be able to cuddle with him. So all I wanted to do was stay. Stay and hold all I had left to hold.

It took about two hours before I talked myself into leaving. I told myself it would only be a few hours and I would be back and I would get to see little Cotton again. After I summoned the courage I needed to leave my baby there while we went home and got dressed for visitation, I walked away.

The hours that separated my visit with Cotton and the open visitation for guests actually flew by. I was amazed to see how our lives were able to escape for a moment or two and we were able to take a breath. A real breath. We were able to get Colt and Cason ready and we did it without breaking down. I guess seeing my little ones all cleaned up and ready helped me to take a step forward.

As people showed up at the funeral home, we hugged them and visited. Again, I was in awe of all God's people around us. My little two-year old had so many people there to see him. I couldn't believe it.

There was laughter, and love, and smiles. Yes, there were tears from all of the guests too, but there was so much life there as well.

Every few moments, I would look around and see people enjoying one another again. I was able to see how God was taking something so painful and turning it into something that would bring Him glory.

So also you have sorrow now, but I will see you again,
and your hearts will rejoice,
and no one will take your joy from you.
John 16:22

People looked at me weirdly as I smiled at them without tears in my eyes.

"How are you doing it? How are you not falling apart?" they would ask.

I responded, "How could I not smile when I have all this love in the room and Cotton is here too? I can go touch him and see him at any moment. But I truly believe it's really just something called God's grace. God prepared us, so I know we will be okay."

I glanced around the room and saw Jordan with tears running down his face. It made me sad to see him hurt so much. Jordan continued to question why we had to endure all this and whether or not he could have done anything to prevent this. He had never really showed his emotions, but when he saw so many that loved us enough to come to see us when we hurt, he allowed himself to feel. He let himself grieve and let himself feel the love that we experienced from these people. We were being held up in prayer and held up in person. We were able to see what we had heard so many times in church. We were seeing God's love being poured out by these people and it overwhelmed Jordan.

When my sisters came in, I reminded them to breathe as they walked in to see Cotton. That was the one thing I forgot to do when I saw Cotton for the first time. I knew they would too. It was hard to see him so still. It was hard to imagine that he would never laugh, play, or run again. It seemed like the only way to see him in that kind of restful state was to hold your breath and wait for him to giggle or smile, but he would never do that again. So we had to remember to breathe.

All the kids went outside and played until it was time to go home. By the time everyone left, it was getting late. As I slowly walked back in to see Cotton, the realization that I would have to leave him here again overwhelmed me and I didn't want to go.

I thought, "Please don't make me leave. I don't want to leave my baby."

But I knew I had to. I knew that this was only part of the process and that I would be able to see him again in the morning. So, I whispered to Cotton that I would see him in the morning. I gave him one last rub as I quickly walked away, trying unsuccessfully to control my sobbing.

That night, Jordan and I talked again. Something was bothering him. So, I asked what was wrong.

He said, "You're doing so good. I don't want to tell you and bring you down."

I told him, "Please tell me; you won't bring me down."

After a minute, he finally said that he couldn't stop thinking about that day. He said that the images were constantly creeping back into his mind. They seemed to invade his thoughts and corrupt his ability to think clearly. He said he was constantly reminded of the fact that his greatest fear had come true and that there was nothing that he could do about it. And even though he knew that there was nothing he could have done, he kept replaying the events in his mind trying to figure out what he might have done to prevent the loss of his little boy. The thoughts pierced his mind and threatened to make a lasting home there.

Knowing that I only had a moment to support my husband, I took it and tried to hold him up before God, with every healing word that I had heard from the Lord that week.

I told him, "You have to let it go. God would have taken Cotton no matter what we did. He had every chance to give Cotton back to us, but He didn't. It was time for Cotton to go to his Heavenly Father. Whether it was the pool that day or the highway the next week or the train tracks in a year, God still would have taken

Cotton from us. You have to accept that and don't let Satan keep those thoughts of guilt in your head. When I start to replay that day, I stop and say, "NO, SATAN, you won't win with me! God, take these thoughts away. And He does."

He hugged me and said, "Thank you, I love you. You are so strong."

I replied, "I may be strong today, but tomorrow I won't be. I'll need you to be the strong one tomorrow."

He smiled and we held one another while we cried ourselves to sleep once more.

Tuesday, July 16, 2013

The morning of the funeral was like any other. The sun rose, and so did we. I got my two boys ready and we tried desperately to get dressed for such a serious event without flooding our house with tears even before we got to the church.

This was the day we had been preparing for all week, but now that it was here, I just didn't really know how I was going to make it through. I tried to stay busy getting the boys into their clothes.

I was completely focused on the kids and the awkwardness of getting ready for an event that I didn't ever think I would attend, when I saw Jordan standing there in a suit. Jordan came out of the bedroom and he stood in the doorway half embarrassed for wearing the suit and half aware of how dapper he looked. For a moment, I was taken away. I was so used to seeing him in dirty work clothes that I almost didn't recognize him. I was thrust back to a time before all this; a time when we weren't planning a funeral for our two-year-old son.

I must have looked kind of silly because he asked me what I was looking at. I was startled by the question because I was staring. Jordan says I blushed when he asked, but I don't think that was true. I was just really proud to see my man looking so good. It almost softened the mood a little. Almost.

After our family arrived, we loaded into cars and made the all too familiar drive to church. We drove that way so many times before that it was hard to recognize the seriousness of that particular day.

As we neared the church, I could remember the first time I laid eyes on that building. I was so afraid back then. I was so scared that people would judge me and condemn me for who I had been. Never in a million years would I have thought I would be here today. I never imagined then that I would be able to bury my son today without an ounce of fear.

We made our way into the building and I immediately looked for Cotton. I found him at the front of the church, but his casket was closed. I immediately started crying. I knew that this was going to be hard and I knew I would need to say goodbye, but the closed casket made it all too real.

I thought, "NO, I'm not ready to say goodbye! I

want to see you, touch you!"

I found the funeral director and asked to see Cotton. After they opened the casket, I rubbed Cotton's little head.

I spoke to him softly, "Hey, baby, I'm here. I don't know if I can get through this day. I can't let you go and never see or touch you again. I already let go of your spirit. I don't know if I can let go of your body. I love you so much. I hope you like the service we picked out for you. I love you bunches."

After another rub on the head, I let them close the casket for the service.

The family gathered in the dining hall while the guests were seated in the worship center. Such a fitting place to have a funeral really. We were going to celebrate the short life of my son and give praise to a God who loved us enough to sacrifice His son so that I could one day see my baby again.

We got lined up and made our way to the sanctuary. There were people everywhere. Our worship center holds over three hundred people and we didn't have enough seats. The church was so full that people were standing along the walls and hallway. They were all here to say goodbye. They were all here because they loved my boy and they loved us.

When the service started, Brother Jimmy talked and read the obituary. You could hear sniffles constantly, because no one masked their sadness. There wasn't a dry eye in the entire place.

After Brother Jimmy finished he nodded his head at me. I had written something for the funeral. I wanted to share my love for my son so that the congregation could see how special this baby was, but now that it was time, my nerves and the pain of letting Cotton go threatened to muffle my voice. I said a quick prayer, "Lord, please let me get through this where they can understand me through my tears."

> June 2nd 2011, God gave us a baby boy
> With big brown eyes
> And a smile that would touch the sky.
> We fell in love with his energy and laughter
> And promised we would always look after.
> We planned to be together forever,
> But God's plans would interfere.
> Two years just wasn't enough.
> We are selfish and want to give you more love.
> We asked God to bring you back to me,
> But instead, He put you on His knee.
> I don't understand why He needed you.
> Now my world is so blue.
> Smiles turned into tears.
> Our joys have turned into fears.
> But when I look up at night,
> I can see that God was right.
> So, I'll be grateful for the memories we made.

And I won't be afraid.
God's love is all around me,
But letting go won't be easy.
Cotton, stay on God's knee
And talk to me.
Send me kisses every day
So you won't feel so far away.
It won't be much longer 'til I can see your face
And hold you close to feel you are safe.
We love you, Cotton,
And you will never be forgotten.

    I sat back down and they played the short video with pictures and videos of Cotton that flashed with a song called "Beautiful Boy" by Coleen McMahon. I cried and cried. I had put together those photos, but seeing them roll across the screen brought back the joy of those days, which only proved to intensify the sadness I was experiencing. At the end of the video, there was an image of a bird flying toward the sky. In my head, I could see Cotton flying home. The idea that he was now with Jesus made the scene bearable, and knowing that he would never again feel pain helped to relieve my pain. I cried some more while Jordan held me tight.
    Brother Jimmy spoke again. Tina Terry, a close church friend, finished the service by singing a song called "Held" by Natalie Grant. After she was seated, the funeral director opened up Cotton's casket and let

people come hug us and say their good-byes to Cotton. I don't even remember what they said. I just remember feeling lifted up by ever hug and every encouraging word. Friends, family, and even some of Cotton's nurses were all there, and I just couldn't believe it. It gave me hope, strength, and the feeling that it was going to be okay. After everyone went by, it was time to go to the burial site.

Jordan had hoped to carry Cotton's casket himself, but I asked him if we could ask for someone else to help because I knew it would be heavy and he had already carried such a heavy burden that day. I didn't want him to assume that he would have to carry that load as well. I wanted to be a helpmate in that situation, but knew that I wasn't the person for that job. We agreed to ask his dad to help him if he needed it. So Jordan and his dad carried Cotton's casket to the car.

The people who wanted to go to the gravesite got in their cars and started to line up. There was a limo to take the close family members. Our tears dried on the six-mile drive to the cemetery, but the evidence was still there. The mood was lighter and we even laughed at times on the way, but the heaviness of the day continued to linger.

When we got to the gravesite, Jordan and his father carried Cotton to the grave where he would be buried. I had never really noticed how much of a burden Jordan carried that day until I saw he and his father take hold of that casket for the last time. I saw three generations of my husband's family walking together, the tragedy of which was that the youngest had passed on, while those who remained bore a sorrow that could never be explained. Jordan stood alongside his father while this tiny casket threatened to crush him. Men should bury their fathers and grandfathers. Not the other way around.

Brother Jimmy said a few short words and everyone stood around and visited as the funeral home released two white doves. I walked back to the limo and cried.

"How am I supposed to just leave him here? I won't be able to rub his head again. This is really happening and I hate it." I ducked my head and I cried some more.

My grandmother saw me get into the limo and came to comfort me. She lost one of her daughters just a year before. She held me close and we cried together.

I heard the car door open. I looked up and wiped my tears.

Jordan said, "Did you want to see him be lowered?"

I shook my head, yes, and I hopped out of the limo and walked back over to Cotton.

I laid a hand on his casket and I prayed, "This is it - my final goodbye. God, please give me strength to let him go. I love you, Cotton. I will see you soon. I promise."

And down he went. I took a deep breath and

walked back to the limo.

I thought, "It's done. I will keep your memories close forever, but tomorrow we will start trying to find our new normal."

Grief, Love, and Moving Forward

The next day, Jordan went back to work. Jordan loved to work, so I knew that he wasn't trying to escape into his job. He loved how work made him feel and he had a great relationship with many of the people with whom he worked. Those people also made it easier to let him go back day after day. I could see how he was able to heal when he worked hard. He was providing for his family and he knew that by doing this, he was honoring God.

It had been so nice to have him home, but the truth was, we couldn't stay home forever. We had to restart life again. It was hard to move past the funeral because it was such a final representation of how we had to keep moving forward. We dove back into our schedules and that helped us to move through many of those first hours.

In spite of our efforts to return to what we knew to be our normal lives, our lives were nothing like they were before we lost Cotton. They were a little quieter and they were a little less busy. The emptiness of our home was a constant reminder to the boys and me. We were able to notice when it was Cotton's turn in the conversation, or when we were so used to hearing him play. It just wasn't there anymore.

Since the accident, Cason had not slept well at all. He seemed to be so aware of the empty bed in the room. He didn't say much about it, but Jordan and I could tell that he was being worn down by the absence of his little brother and the knowledge that Cotton would never come back.

It was so hard for me to see the empty bed too and the closet full of clothes that he would never again use. Each thing was a reminder of how we had lost something special in our lives. I didn't let my mind wonder about what he would have been like when he grew up or how he might have acted. I just tried to refocus on the wonderful memory of Cotton's life rather than the tragedy of his death.

So the day Jordan went back to work, I started working on removing these reminders from our lives. I took the bed down and put it away in the basement. I gathered his scattered clothes and packed up most of his stuff. I made a pile of things he would have outgrown to sell in an upcoming garage sale and made a pile of keepsake items to be put in special places.

I was careful to keep the things that were most significant to Cotton. I wanted to make sure that he was represented in our home and in the way we walked through life. I kept his tractors, because they were his favorite toys, and I put them up high in the closet. I saved his big stuffed animals because he loved to snuggle with them and they reminded me of how much he loved everyone around him.

I had some of my favorite pictures of Cotton blown up and hung them in the playroom and living room, and I hung the handprints the hospital sent next to one of the pictures. I wanted my boys to be able to sleep without the constant reminder of their loss, but I wanted to remind them of their baby brother when they played, when they laughed, and when they could look at his big smile and remember how much they loved him.

It was all about perspective. I wanted to let the boys know that it was good to remember and that it was even good to be reminded of their loss, but it was not healthy to lay awake at night and wallow in grief. We had to live and we couldn't do that if we didn't begin to move on.

I picked out my favorite clothes of Cottons and had a memory bear made out of them. It was just a little Teddy Bear made completely out of Cotton's clothes, but it was such a blessing for Colt. He would take "Cotton Bear" and tuck him into Cason's bed when it was Colt's naptime so they could take naps together, just like when Cotton was alive. Colt struggled so much with how alone he felt, but that little bear filled his heart just a little bit.

Everything I did for the next few weeks was about healing. I took the boys places to help them heal and Jordan and I talked for hours at times just to help restore each other. We each processed our emotions in a different way and one of the ways that I was able to reconcile my emotions was to journal my thoughts, prayers, and feelings.

I knew a lot of people wondered how I would be doing during the weeks following Cotton's death. I updated my Facebook status to let them know what I felt God had told me and shown me through the days. These posts are exactly as I wrote them. No editing was done because I wanted you to know how close the Lord was to me during those days and how He made His way closer as my pain grew stronger.

```
     July 18th: I keep asking, how am
I doing so good? Why is it that I
can smile and laugh to the mention of
Cotton's name when so many cry? I try
to think about being upset and crying
and mad.... but then I hear Cotton
laugh... And remember how good it felt to
be his mom... and of course, I have my
```

boys who still need their functioning mom... But the only answer I came across is that it's God's grace... He takes the ugly memories, pain, and sadness and leaves happiness, loving memories, and joy... I know I'll have moments ...maybe even full days... but if I have learned anything... it's that God does get u thru it... if you haven't found Him... please find Him... because I walked with Him at least a full year before this awful moment. And it's as if He is sitting here next to me saying, "It's OK!" I never once was mad at God... I did scream to bring Cotton back, but not mad. He chose to keep him... only because I know how awesome Cotton is... so I'd be selfish and keep him too ... all of y'all's prayers are part of this healing too... y'all's love for my family has been a blessing... we love y'all so much! Thank you... I can't say it enough.

July 22: How do u do it? they ask.. My answer.. You take it day by day... hold the memories close and the pictures closer... Pray to God every day... and try to find your new normal... It has been a little over a week since Cotton left me... and it feels like a lifetime ago.. It doesn't feel like Cotton has left this world... he's just staying with a close loved one 'til I can go get him... How I miss him.. I can't explain the feeling of his presence, but yet the longing to hold him, talk to him, and snuggle with him... The day will come… someday soon... and I will get to hold him again... 'Til that day.. I will hold my boys a little closer... and love them more...if that is even possible...

July 27: Losing my Cotton has made me look at my life ... I can accept it was God's plan and He will continue to bless me for the rest of my life and always love Him for it ... or I can crawl in a hole and cry and reject the amazing God that gave my little boy to me then took him from me... I could hate this world for everything I hurt for... but that is Satan, I have decided... I may have tears fall cuz he's not in my back seat talking to me... or not there to cuddle with... but I will not let Satan win me over... I gave my life to God. I am holding Him to His promises He made to me... so in return, I shall keep mine to Him… y'all have a blessed day ..

July 28: You knocked on my heart and I let u in.. I didn't know what was in store for me, but I entrusted you with my life… not understanding the path you have laid out for me .. I still followed the best I could... finding it was hard at times and felt so alone but somehow I made it thru with more than I had before... now as I look back after so many years I can see it.. I see that You taught me before I went thru it, held me when I was going thru it, and blessed me for always keeping You close... you see... He may not be in human form to hold your hand or speak to you, but when you answer His knock, He will steer the way to a blessed life.

August 9: Some days I cry, some days I smile, but all days I know that as soon as my work is done, I get to go home... so I shall preach the word, love everyone the way Jesus loves me, and wait 'til He calls me home... that's what we have to look forward to... Satan is around every corner... you can let him drive... or throw him out of the car each time... for me… I shall allow God to drive even when it's hard ... love y'all!

August 11: Meredith Andrews "Start with Me" song. I want to make a difference.. I want to prove that God is enough... I want Him to start with me, to show the world that He is all we need.... I fell in love with this song before the accident and now I feel God has given me my "start"! Hope y'all enjoy.

August 14: Learn to enjoy life, relax, and remember that I am God with you. I crafted you with enormous capacity to know Me and enjoy my presence. When my ppl wear sour faces and walk through their lives with resigned rigidity, I am displeased. When u walk through a day with childlike delight savoring every blessing, you proclaim your trust in Me, your ever present Shepherd. The more you focus on My presence with you, the more fully you can enjoy life...

Yesterday was a hard day... but God never fails me.... sometimes words can't explain the way He holds me.. or the way He can take my pain and fill it with something else... the way He can push the devil away from me when I struggle... I just seem to cry in awe of how much He loves me...

August 16: One of the most frustrating things in this world is people are so focused on the negative and unfairness instead of all the beauty and blessings they have received... this world is ugly... but when you focus on God and His light... I guess you will see it differently then... God bless and be happy..

August 28: Too many think that following God is supposed to make life easy and more comfortable. They are looking for a God of convenience. The truth is that it often takes hard work to live by God's high standards. He may call us to face poverty or suffering. But if serving God is more important to us than anything else, what we must give up is of little importance compared to what we gain-eternal life with God... so my question is... are you giving to God in full and honestly or are u giving to God the wasted trash because it's convenient??

Throughout those months, people still came over to hug and visit with us, and as usual, with every hug I felt that much stronger. They still asked how I was not falling apart or not mad because I didn't have Cotton with me. I gave them the same answer, "God's grace holds me." Cotton brought so much joy to my life. I am so thankful God chose me to be his mother. I could never be upset because of all God has provided me.

Because I asked God to take my pain away, He did. He filled my emptiness with joy and love through all the people that surrounded me. How can I be mad at that? He promised me that I would be with Cotton forever; I just have to live here in this broken world without him for a little while. That is the joy of our salvation, that we know that we are promised eternity. I was not promised a pain free life, I was promised that through His pain on the cross, I can be free from sin and death to live with Jesus forever!

> *Jesus said to her, "I am the resurrection and the life. Whoever believes in me, though he die, yet shall he live, and everyone who lives and believes in me shall never die. Do you believe this? John 11:25-26*

I knew that my salvation was real and I saw how the Lord had changed my life in so many ways. I knew that what he said about eternity was real. I believed that Jesus was raised from the dead, so my faith that I would be reunited with Cotton was easy in comparison.

Everyone Grieves in Their Own Way

So many people in our church and in our small community had loved Cotton, so they had to figure out how they were going to get back to normal life too. Returning to life meant that we could never forget. We could never forget how much Cotton meant to so many people and one of the ways that some people tried to show their support to us was that they gave money to our church in Cotton's name. A memorial fund had been set up for Cotton.

The Ropes High School girls' basketball team had a fundraiser for us and the community was so supportive. When they gave the money to us, we put it into the Cotton Memorial fund at our church.

Almost immediately, we thought of using the money to build a new playground at our church. Cotton loved our church and we loved to have him there playing and running. We thought it could be a great way for our church to experience the memory of Cotton, too. We wanted it to be a place where children could enjoy the fellowship of church, even though they didn't quite know what that was just yet.

My brother-in-law had window decal stickers made of a cotton boll and a halo on top. We passed those out to everyone who wanted one and everyone who donated to the Cotton memorial fund. I really enjoy driving through town and seeing Cotton's sticker on cars. I just sat and smiled as I saw Cotton's face smiling back at me. The sticker didn't just symbolize Cotton to me; it was a reminder of faith, grace, and love too. It reminded me that, even though losing Cotton was the worst feeling in the world, my relationship with God was how I was able to overcome the ugly feelings.

My mom made a t-shirt blanket out of all of cotton's special t-shirts. It was about the size of a baby blanket because he was so young. He didn't have that many important shirts and the ones he had were so small. My mom had a couple of his pictures printed on fabric to add to what she had, which made it that much more special. It had all the shirts that the grandparents got for him and represented how much Cotton was loved by those in our family. They got to see the blanket and remember how they had invested into his life. Not that getting someone a t-shirt makes that much of a difference. It's that they are reminded of how important he was and how they were part of growing him for the years we had him.

My mom was honored that she got to be a part of making some of his memorial. She said there were a lot of tears sewn into the blanket. It was good for her to be able to invest herself into his memory around our house. Her making this blanket helped me remember that many people lost Cotton, not just Jordan and me. My eyes were opened to the fact that people grieve in different ways and they respond to death in different ways. I got to work on the boys' rooms and I got to have the pool taken down. I got to plan a funeral and bury my son. I was able to grieve in my own way and I was being healed by God throughout the process. I needed that.

Others needed to invest some of their money into a playground and others needed to raise money to support us. Others needed to make things with their hands to remind themselves of how much love they had for Cotton. We all had to grieve, we all had to grow, we all had to take steps toward living without this sweet little man, and God helped us all do that. In fact, God used our situation to display his love and compassion.

We had people come to our church and rededicate their lives to Christ. The reason they gave for their recommitment was because of how they saw God represented in Jordan and me. Each time we heard this testimony, I was so amazed that God could use me. It hadn't been that long ago that I was a person that nobody wanted to be like. Sometimes, in fact, I didn't even want to be like me, but with God, I was transformed into someone different. I couldn't have done any of that myself and I was constantly reminded of that. My strength was never enough to change, nor was it ever enough to live without my baby, but through Christ, I was able to be a new creature.

Other people saw what God was doing in our lives and in our city and wanted a part of that, too. They wanted to know what the love of God was really like and they hungered for a relationship with Him. They didn't envy what we had to go through, but they were able to see how, in a circumstance that was terrible, my God was greater.

That's when I realized a miracle had been done for me and for those around me. God used Cotton's death and our reaction to it to touch hundreds of lives. If God had chosen to return Cotton to us, we would have been eternally grateful, but instead, he used us to grow his kingdom and changed the eternity of countless people. That is the most uplifting and healing thought of all. My baby is in heaven with Jesus and others will be arriving soon because of his story!

I knew God didn't want me to suffer and hurt,

but this is a broken world and death is a real part of it. God was able to show me how much he loved me throughout this situation by changing the destination of some who were spiritually dead. God helped to heal me by showing me that He takes the things that are intended for evil and redeems them for His purpose.

As for you, you meant evil against me,
but God meant it for good, to bring it about that many
people should be kept alive, as they are today.
Genesis 50:20

Healing the Brokenhearted

*D*ays turned into weeks, weeks turned to months, and months turned into seasons. The height of the summer rush for Jordan's company began to dwindle and the rush of the harvest season began to build. Our days were shorter, nights were longer, and our hearts were stronger. Our lives were different, but the difference was becoming more normal.

Jordan and I still spent hours talking at night, but from time to time, our conversation would begin to cover topics other than Cotton's death, the way our lives were different or how much we hurt. We began to talk about life again. We spoke of the sons we were still raising and the lives we were still living. We spoke of upcoming events with joy at times and we talked about plans for our future. We learned how to share ourselves with one another, again, and maybe even better than we ever did before.

One of our consistent points of discussion was how well Cason and Colt were dealing with Cotton's loss and the new life we were living without him. We worked hard to help them remember how much they loved Cotton and how they will miss him, in a healthy way. That was a lot harder than I thought it would be because their ability to understand emotion and the spiritual blessings we were seeing around us was so much more limited than an adult's. Nevertheless, we worked on it almost every night.

Throughout the fall, Cason struggled to understand all that he was feeling and all that the loss of his brother would do to change his life. Cason acted out in school and at home, lashed out at people, back-talked everyone, was very disrespectful, and was angry whenever he didn't get his way.

Any time we asked what was wrong and why he acted that way, his response was always, "I don't know."

As frustrating as it was to hear him say that he didn't know why he was so angry or why he was so hateful to others, I knew it was true. He didn't know. He didn't know why he felt so hostile because the idea of grief and sadness couldn't quite be separated from the feelings of anger and retaliation. He was hurt and more often than not, hurting people hurt other people.

We would have long conversations about what he was feeling and talk about how our actions had to be kind, even if we didn't feel happy inside. I had to drag the answer out of him, but he finally told me, "I just miss Cotton."

It was so sad to hear him say this and it only served to help me be patient with him. It was a little easier to discuss his actions with him after that point. He knew that there was a reason for the way he felt, but also knew he still had a responsibility to act correctly at home and at school.

After many discussions about how we cannot behave in that manner just because we miss someone, things would get better for that day. Cason slowly became less angry and disrespectful. He started to quit feeling sorry for himself for losing Cotton. He started living life again.

ೞ ೞ ೞ

Long before any of this had happened, we planned to buy a dog for our boys. We lived in the country and we knew that a dog would be a great thing for our boys. What better way, we thought, for a boy to grow up, than to have a dog? But more than that, Cotton loved dogs. He loved them almost as much as he loved tractors. So to get a dog for the family was a good thing, but we knew that this dog would belong to Cotton. So we set out to find the perfect dog for Cotton.

We knew the things we wanted in a dog and did a lot of research to find the perfect dog for our family. We knew that finding the best fit for our family would help to ensure that we could fit this new dog into what we were already doing. As we talked about good qualities in a dog, we noticed that a few things kept coming up.

- Good-natured
- Good with kids
- Not aggressive
- Large
- Protector
- Male

We knew we wanted a male dog because Jordan demanded only one thing on our getting-a-dog checklist. Jordan had this idea that if we were to have a daughter, or even a girl puppy, that he would immediately begin to age at a more rapid pace. He constantly would say that he didn't want grey hair just yet, but I really think it was that a little girl scared him to death, so he used gray hair as an excuse.

The breed we finally chose was a South African Boerboel and we found a breeder in the Dallas Area who had a great reputation for producing elite dogs which fit all of our wish list. We saw some photos that were emailed to us and it was love at first sight. We knew we wanted one of these beautiful dogs and couldn't wait to get him.

We ordered Zeus from the breeders in November of 2012, but we didn't tell the kids just in case the deal fell through. We wanted them to be surprised by the dog, and since we didn't even know when he would arrive, we didn't want them to get their hopes up and be hurt by not getting one. The first litter was born, but there were no males.

So, we waited for the second litter to be born. The breeder called us and told us that it would be a little longer than expected because their dog had a false pregnancy. I started to think this was a joke and this breeder was a phony, but after Jordan convinced me to be patient, we were told that another litter would be born sometime in June, 2013.

In this litter, there was a male and the breeder sent us pictures and kept us posted through the first months of our dog's progress. August 17, 2013 we made a fast trip to Dallas to pick up our new family member. The boys were so excited once they found out we would get to take this puppy home.

There was a little sparkle of joy in the kids' eyes again. They got to enjoy this new dog and it softened the blow of losing a brother. The boys laughed the whole way home. They thought this puppy was the greatest thing on the planet and they loved to sit and pet him and couldn't wait to play with him.

It amazed me how God's plan worked out so perfectly. We waited so long for this dog and it amazed me that God was able to bring him into our lives at the right moment. God knew when our boys would be ready to accept this puppy and Zeus came to us just at the right time. Timing was everything. I saw how

Cason had been so angry for so long and how he would occasionally let his guard down when he was around Zeus. I saw how Jordan and I were able to sit and watch our boys play again. God used that little puppy to give us a break from the constant pain of our loss.

Being only three years old at the time, Colt connected to Zeus from the first moment, and we couldn't have planned a better connection if we wanted to. Colt had a buddy again. When Colt would go play in the mud, Zeus laid next to him and sometimes would help dig too. They would lay outside and relax. They would run around our property and go on little adventures.

Before we got Zeus, Colt would try to be around Cason nearly all the time. He had been so accustomed to being with Cotton all day, every day that he struggled to understand the idea that he didn't have someone to play with throughout the day. Cason, on the other hand, had spent so much time as an only child, not to mention that Colt and Cotton were so close from the beginning, he had never really been bothered by their little boy shenanigans. But now, Colt wanted someone to play with and Zeus finally filled that gap. Cason got to go back to being the big brother rather than the playmate of a three-year-old.

With a puppy in the house, Colt didn't seem to have to be in Cason's face the whole day. So Cason got a little bit of a break from being big brother all the time.

Colt didn't seem to be so lonely after we got Zeus. He had a friend again. Someone who could be there at any moment and play just how Colt wanted to play. Little by little, Colt returned to the fun-loving little boy he used to be.

Each day, I was reminded of the healing Zeus brings to us all - how he always licked Colt when he woke up, just like when the boys would hug after naps. When Colt took a bath, Zeus demanded that he be next to the tub to watch and play. Zeus enjoyed being outside with the boys and playing with them.

Getting this dog was one of the best ways we could have continued to heal that fall. We needed a distraction and we needed a companion. He helped us all in one way or another. From helping Jordan reconnect at times with Cason and Colt, to laying next to me as I cried, Zeus was the perfect representation of normal that we could have asked for. He let us live again. He demanded that we engage again. He called us to run through life with joy again.

෪ ෪ ෪

I started Christmas shopping in October and actually completed it by the second week of November. I knew that these holidays right after a tragic accident weren't going to be easy, and I wanted to stay focused on my family's ability to see the joy of these holidays, instead of constantly feeling sorry for something that we had just experienced. One of the ways that I wanted to do that was to have the mundane things out of the way long before we got to the event. I wanted our family to focus on each other, not the emptiness in the room. I wanted them to center their attention on the Love we received from our Lord Jesus Christ, not the lies that Satan was going to hurl our way. I wanted us to focus on the important parts of the holidays themselves.

For Thanksgiving, I wanted us to give thanks in all that we did and have. I wanted to be thankful for having such wonderful people in my life and give back to them if I could. I wanted to be reminded of all that we have in our salvation, our church, our community, and our family. I wanted to feel gratitude for the fact that I was here, and able to share love and hope with other people.

Back in 2011, I started a tradition for Thanksgiving where I cooked for all of our family who lived close by. Since most of the Gregg family was still harvesting cotton in the fields, they never really had a Thanksgiving dinner. So that year, and thereafter, I cooked and hosted Thanksgiving at my house.

I enjoyed cooking all the food and having the family over and it was a great way to get to see people that you usually didn't get to see during that season. Cotton harvesting was such an important part of our lives that I never considered the family stopping the harvest for a day off. Instead, I wanted to bless them in all their work by giving them a few hours to enjoy the fruits of their labor and hopefully, be grateful to the God who gave them all these things.

But in 2013, it was a little different. I didn't want the holidays to be depressing because of Cotton leaving us, so I was determined to keep a smile on my face and try to make sure everyone was having a good time. Maybe it was painted on at times and maybe I didn't feel as joyous as I made myself out to be, but I wanted to focus on Thanksgiving, not mourning.

Jordan cooked the turkey for his family and I made almost everything else. For the most part, everyone seemed okay, and there were only a few references to how quiet the house was, or how sad it was to have an empty seat, and that made for a fairly normal gathering of Jordan's family. The mood was light, but I could feel a level of tension. I really never expected it to be carefree, so the air of dissatisfaction was tolerable.

Cason wanted to play dominoes, so the grandparents stayed for a round of "train." They seemed to enjoy the game and they even let go a little while playing. It was good for them to interact with Cason and good for him to see them smile. The sadness of the day was overshadowed by the thankfulness we all felt for what we had right in front of us.

That weekend, we had a family reunion for my mom's side of the family. We do it every year and it was good to see my family get together again. One thing I love most about my mom's family is they are all very loud and they all enjoy laughing. Sometimes, we even had to wrestle down an uncle or aunt or even cousins just to be silly, but there was always laughter in the air. Maybe it was because Thanksgiving was a day or two in the past or maybe it was because we had already seen how thankful we all were for those who were in our lives or maybe it was yet another blessing from the Holy Spirit, but that weekend did more to heal my heart than I can really even know. I was able to cut loose and relax, which was something that I needed, but hadn't really had time to do.

෫ ෫ ෫

Christmas is the celebration of the birth of our King and the fact that our church worked so hard to celebrate Christmas made it easier to focus our eyes on the gift of Jesus instead of the loss of Cotton. By this time, I was so ready to start telling people how much healing God had done in my life that I wanted to show as many people, kids, and even strangers the real meaning of Christmas. I wanted them to know the great news of salvation in Jesus Christ. I wanted them to know what brought me joy, even though my Cotton was gone. I wanted them to see how I could have joy. My joy was because of the fact that through Jesus, I would get to see my baby one day. Through Jesus, I can have life forever.

So, when I went shopping for Christmas, I knew

it would be hard not to look at the clothes that Cotton would wear or look at some of the toys I might have purchased for him. I knew it might be hard to see these things and not be overwhelmed with sadness, so I made a plan before I ever went into the store. I had one less child I had to buy for that Christmas, but God had still blessed me with the ability to love and share His treasure with others.

Our Church collected names each year of families in our community and in the surrounding area that might not have a Christmas at all. Each child's information was placed on a card and available to anyone in our church who wanted to share the joy of giving gifts to someone else. I knew that was my opportunity. I knew that was a way for me to show the love I had for Jesus to a child who wouldn't otherwise have much that year. When Jordan and I got the names out of the stack, we selected three boys from three to twelve years of age. I bought two outfits, pajamas, two toys, bathroom supplies, and a Bible for each of them.

I wanted these kids to know the joy of Christmas, but I also wanted them to remember their presents throughout the year. This way, these kids would have something to remind them that they were loved longer than a few days playing with a new toy. I got the Bible because I knew they might be open to hear the Gospel because they had been shown kindness and the thought of giving them earthly things was nice, but the thought of helping them choose Jesus for eternity was extremely exciting.

Christmas week came quickly, yet again, and I didn't want to have a depressing holiday because Cotton left us. I wanted this to be a special time to remember all that God had done for us and to remember Cotton in a special way too. I knew there was nothing that I could buy anyone that would help them remember Cotton, so I tried to make as many things as I could that would be special gifts to each family member and could remind each of them about how much they loved little Cotton.

First, we went to Jordan's grandmother's house. I made her a collage of Cotton's black and white pictures on giant puzzle pieces because she liked to do puzzles. Not only was it a great gift for her to be able to use many times, it was a way for her to remember her great-grandchild as often as she wanted.

Then came time for my parents' Christmas. The whole family was there and everyone was happy as usual. All seven of the grand-boys were running around playing and the deafening noise was music to my ears. There was so much joy in the air and we celebrated. We really celebrated like there was something good to be celebrating. That is the Christmas joy that I was waiting for. The opportunity to have to ask someone to speak louder because we were all laughing too hard or the ability to stuff yourself full of food and sit back and giggle at stories you've heard a thousand times. It was a good time and it only added to how special the gifts were for my family.

When it was time for presents, the kids always opened first. They got their toys and went to work with them as soon as they had the chance, but the presents I was most ready for were to my parents.

I had gotten my dad a knife that said "we love you grandpa" and a money clip with Cotton's symbol and his dates. For my mom, I made her a large fancy photo album of all the pictures I had of Cotton. Just about every memory I had of Cotton was in this book. As she held it and cried, I told her that only she, my mother-in-law, and I have this book. I wanted to share my everyday memories with her since Cotton was a "grandma's boy," but also so she could share Cotton's joy with whoever would listen. It was a reminder that the memories we have are far more precious than the time we lost. We were able to remember the little boy who smiled so much in a time where there were a lot of smiles to be shared.

If your family is anything like ours, you know that Christmastime is a marathon, not a sprint. We still had one family get-together to attend and that was Jordan's family. So the next day, we had a pajama Christmas, so everyone wore their pajamas. The air was different here. Since Jordan only had one brother who wasn't married and had no kids, it was just my kids there. Everyone was very quiet and settled. I made my mother-in-law the same photo album of Cotton and requested the same thing from her, to share Cotton with whoever would listen. For my father-in-law, I got him a John Deere knife and a money clip with Cotton's symbol and dates.

On Christmas Eve night, Santa came to see the boys. I was always so excited to see their faces the next morning when they saw that Santa came. Christmas morning, the boys got up and were just as excited as ever. I was excited for them and enjoyed watching them rip open each present they had received. Once everything was open, Dad had the job of helping put toys together. It was a great time for them. The boys loved their presents and getting to play with their dad was the icing on the cake.

Cotton came to my mind several times that day. All I could think was, "Merry Christmas, sweet boy." It was hard to not see him opening presents this year, but I was determined to not let his absence mess up the spirit of Christmas. So, I played with Cason and Colt and I smiled as we built toys together, ate great food, and loved each other that day.

One Year Later

At some point in time during the spring of 2014, I started to think about the fact that we would celebrate some major milestones and anniversaries for Cotton's life and Cotton's death. At first, I didn't know how to feel about them. I continued to have good days and bad days as I missed my little boy, but I trusted that God would give me the strength and stability that I would need to endure these events just like He did with all the things that we had already walked through.

The three most important events that we would be encountering were the dedication of Cotton's memorial playground, the celebration of his birthday without him, and the anniversary of his death. In a matter of about 40 days, we would have to endure each of these and I struggled to know how I should feel about them.

I knew I wanted to celebrate Cotton's life and I knew that I would want him to be remembered as the fun-loving toddler that he was, but I also knew that seeing all these things and walking through each of these days would take its toll on me and my family. So, how was I going to do it? How was I going to celebrate God's blessing of Cotton's life without the shadow of his death overpowering me?

Even though I walk through the valley of the shadow of death, I will fear no evil, for you are with me;
Psalm 23:4a

I made a plan to try to be as celebratory as I could possibly be without neglecting the reality of our loss. Jordan and I agreed that we would try to function as great parents for Cason and Colt and we would attempt to love each other throughout this painful period of time as husband and wife. We planned the dedication and we planned the birthday party. We planned the days that we would spend together on the anniversary of that most dreadful day. We planned everything we could and placed our faith in the Holy Spirit to walk us through.

But as we planned, Satan planned too.

I heard once that Satan's attacks are like arrows shot from a bow. It is as though he stands back and flings insults, pain, and doubt at us trying to pierce through the faith we have in God. Our defenses against these attacks are listed in the scripture.

> [10] *Finally, be strong in the Lord and in the strength of his might.* [11] *Put on the whole armor of God, that you may be able to stand against the schemes of the devil.* [12] *For we do not wrestle against flesh and blood, but against the rulers, against the authorities, against the cosmic powers over this present darkness, against the spiritual forces of evil in the heavenly places.* [13] *Therefore take up the whole armor of God, that you may be able to withstand in the evil day, and having done all, to stand firm.* [14] *Stand therefore, having fastened on the belt of truth, and having put on the breastplate of righteousness,* [15] *and, as shoes for your feet, having put on the readiness given by the gospel of peace.* [16] *In all circumstances take up the shield of faith, with which you can extinguish all the flaming darts of the evil one;* [17] *and take the helmet of salvation, and the sword of the Spirit, which is the word of God…*
> Ephesians 6:10-17

The faith that I had in Jesus and the knowledge of what He has already done to help me overcome the loss of my son is what provided me with the most strength as we geared up for these three major events. However, just because I had faith doesn't mean that it wasn't a battle.

The Memorial

As we approached the day for the playground dedication, I began to think that maybe this just wasn't as important to other people as it was to me and that maybe we should just call the whole thing off. I kept having this thought that nobody was going to come and that it was selfish of me to expect people to celebrate a project at our church, but every time I got close to canceling the service, I heard the Lord remind me that His people needed this day.

All the money that had been raised for Cotton's memorial had been donated to our little church to help provide a playground. There had been some old swings and a slide that had become a little bit of a liability and needed to be replaced. There had been some work done by church members to try to improve the play area, but there still needed to be a lot of work done.

Jordan and I had decided long before the spring that we wanted to invest into the children's ministry of our church by using the memorial money to build a playground, so we went to work.

I took lead in finding a good company, deals, and designs. With Jordan working again, it gave my two boys and me plenty of time to find the perfect playground for our church. It took several months to pick the best design and wait for it to go on sale so we could afford it. We wanted to make the donations of our friends and family stretch as far as we could make them go. We wanted to be good stewards of the gift that God had given us.

We finally found a small, family-owned business

that had high quality products. They custom-designed the playground with the descriptions of what I wanted. We tried to design the playground so that as our church continued to grow, it would work in concert with everything else that the Lord had for us.

We settled on a two-level design that had a low level for the younger kids and a higher one for the older kids that was connected by a bridge. We knew that we wanted at least two slides and three or four entryways to get on to it. On a separate structure, we added a swing set with two big kid swings and two bucket seats.

Our local school colors are green, black and white, so we made sure to use those colors so that our community would see it as a place for everyone, not just people who called our church home. The slides were green, the trim white, and the poles were all black.

Once we got the playground ordered, it took about six weeks for it to come in. We had about twelve volunteers from church, family, and community come help put it together. The owner of Playgrounds, Etc. even came and helped us build the playground. It was a cold, windy day, so I felt so bad for all of them, but I was so grateful for their hard work. To complete the area, Jordan and I designed a bench to go in the playground as a dedication to Cotton's memory. We ordered it through the same people that designed Cotton's headstone and it was perfect.

As the days got closer to the dedication service,

I tried to write a speech. I read my speech to Jordan and asked him if he wanted to go to the front with me when I spoke, but since he has a paralyzing fear of public speaking, he generously allowed me to do it all by myself.

I read it to him like I planned to do on the day of the dedication and Jordan said he loved it. He said it was exactly what we needed to say because it was exactly how each of us had been feeling. We were grateful and sad. We were excited to see Cotton again in Heaven, but sad that we don't have him here with us. We were saddened for the fact that we were dedicating a playground in memory of our son, but enthusiastic about what it could mean as a blessing for our church.

I told him that if I got too nervous about standing in front of the group, I might just say, "Thank you all for being here. Now Jordan would like to take over from here and tell you all about this new playground." Then, when I sat back down, Jordan would have no choice but to stand up and say something.

Jordan's eyes immediately filled with fear at the notion that I might really do it and I laughed uncontrollably. He replied, grinning ear to ear, "And I will get up there and say, 'Dannie and I have decided to get a divorce.'" I laughed even harder.

I really wasn't sure how my emotions would play out during this time, but I knew that Jordan would be there for me. I knew that even though he didn't want to speak in front of people, he would move heaven and earth for me to feel supported as I addressed our church.

I felt more nervous about getting up and reading in front of everyone and the sadness of why we were having to have a dedication in the first place. Some people would ask me if it hurt to look at the playground or if it made me sad. My answer was always, "No, not when there were children laughing and playing on it. Or when I catch someone smiling at his picture on the bench. I am encouraged by the fact that we are spreading joy to those people and that makes me feel so much better."

The dedication that Sunday night was simple. We wanted the service to be focused on God and how He loves us and dedicate this new facility to His service. So when it came time to have the service, we started with the video that the funeral home had prepared for Cotton's memorial.

As the song started and a video of Cotton came on, my heart started to rip. I tried to stop crying, but there was no way. Seeing those pictures again made my heart ache for the loss of my baby. My head kept telling me to turn away from the screen so I wouldn't cry, but my heart longed to see the pictures flash across the screen.

Memories of me holding him and hearing him came flooding back and along with the memories came the sorrow of losing him. I kept telling myself that I was not going to cry, but when a picture of me holding

Cotton came to the screen I stopped trying. I stopped trying to hide my sadness and I let myself cry again.

After the videos ended, I blinked back the remaining tears and quickly wiped away the ones that escaped down my face. I looked up at Jordan, who had not even attempted to slow his weeping, and yet again my heart broke because I knew his heart agonized at every picture that flashed across the screen.

I could hear all the sniffles through the church, but Jordan's were the loudest. As Brother Jimmy started to speak, it helped to lighten the mood and most of the tears dried. Then Jeremy led us in some songs about how God had not forgotten us. They were intended to remind us that through Jesus' death on the cross, we will see Cotton again.

I was grateful for the message that Brother Jimmy gave and the songs Jeremy sang because they brought back a lighter atmosphere from where the video had left us. It wasn't lighter because they made light of a serious situation. It was lighter because the knowledge of what Jesus did for us freed us from the sorrow of death and loss. We could rejoice in the fact that our struggle here on earth was short, and that our joy with God in Heaven will be eternal.

Once it was my turn, I got really nervous again, but after I started to read my speech, my nerves settled. In my speech, I selected an excerpt of this book, even though it wasn't finished yet. After I made it back to my seat, Jordan's tears were back full force. I felt helpless; unable to say anything to comfort him, or soften the aching of his broken heart.

Brother Jimmy announced that we would be going outside to cut the ribbon. After everyone made their way out the back door to surround the playground, Brother Jimmy took a moment to pray that God would use this new place to bring joy to children and share the love of Christ with the children of our church and community.

Then, we let Colt cut the ribbon and the kids burst through the gate so that they could play. Everyone walked around and looked at the bench. People took pictures of everything. I just sat and watched in amazement of how God always seems to make something so horrible shine with happiness.

When we got to the house that night, I was glad that we got to do the dedication and that so many cared enough to be there, but I was also glad that it was over. It was one more step that I had overcome with the grace of God by my side. I was reassured that this was a great way for our community and church to continue to heal after our loss. So many people gave to make the playground work and they got to see the Lord be glorified with the money they gave. Satan hoped we would minimize the playground, but God wanted to glorify Himself through His people.

Cotton's 3rd Birthday

For Cotton's third birthday, I struggled to decide whether to invite more of the family over or just keep it between the boys and me. I felt really bad not including everyone, but I also wanted this to be as happy for the boys and us as possible.

Also, after Cotton's second birthday, we had already discussed how Cotton wanted his next cake to look, so when I went to have it made, it brought back the great memory of my little man and how he was so excited about his next birthday. But Satan also took the time to help me remember how much I missed him. Even though the cake would be exactly what Cotton wanted, there was no way for Cotton to celebrate that day, because he was gone.

When I was ordering the cake, the cake decorator asked if I wanted anything written on the cake. I had to fight tears and my voice cracked when I said the words, "Happy Birthday, Cotton."

I quickly put my sunglasses on and I left. Once I found the safety and seclusion of my truck, I wept again. It was so much harder than I could have imagined. Sorrow seemed to creep into my heart and invade my thoughts, but God sent the encouragement of the Holy Spirit to remind me of how this day would be one that celebrated the joy we shared with Cotton and the glory of the God who gave us life.

When June 2nd finally arrived, I knew how I

wanted to spend it and I hoped we would spend it like this every year. I wanted to celebrate the life of Cotton and help my kids remember him. I wanted us to be able to spend some time as a family. I hoped that it could be a time where we continued the healing process and grew a little closer as a family.

The day started as a busy summer day, just like normal. It was filled with basketball camp, grocery shopping, Monday errands, and house cleaning. Jordan worked all day, so we met at the house that evening and made our way to the cemetery. I kept the agenda for the party a surprise. All the kids knew was that there was cake and balloons. They were excited to celebrate Cotton's birthday with cake and balloons, even though he wasn't here.

When we got to the gravesite that afternoon, I instructed Cason and Colt to think about what they wanted to write to Cotton. I found green and yellow balloons and the plan was that each of us would write a little message for Cotton on a balloon and then release them together as a family. Colt and Cason got to choose a color to write their message on and we sat down to write together. I held the balloon while Jordan wrote Colt's message for him and Jordan held Cason's balloon while he wrote his message. I held Jordan's balloon while he wrote his message and Jordan held my balloon while I wrote mine. It was nice that we couldn't do the project alone. We had to work as a family. It was oddly reminiscent of the fact that the struggle over the past year had not been done alone either. We had to lean on each other.

Once we wrote our message on a colored balloon of our choice, we counted to three and let them all go. We watched those balloons rise higher and higher into the sky, every second growing smaller and harder to see. The boys watched as they saw their messages drift farther and farther into the air. Watching those balloons take our love to Cotton helped to remind us that Cotton was in an altogether different place. A place where there was no pain and a place where celebration is constant. It was refreshing to think that he might know how much we loved him, how much we missed him, and be able to see the joy of our reunion coming some day in the future.

It was a sweet moment. There weren't really any tears. Just sadness and a longing to hear Cotton again; but we each knew that we would celebrate that reunion in heaven with God and Cotton.

After watching the balloons go higher and higher, I went to get the cake from the car because a party just isn't the same without cake. It was designed as a cotton field with little green rows on a field of chocolate. It was kind of like the fields of West Texas when cotton first comes out of the ground. It reminded me of Cotton's short life here with us. When cotton first sprouts, it is small and beautiful. It is headstrong and full of life. It bursts out of the earth and changes the way people feel. It changes the way they think. For farmers, cotton is full of life and full of hope. And that is just how we remembered our Cotton.

Rightfully so, a small toy tractor sat on top of the cake along with the words, "Happy Birthday, Cotton."

The words were written in white in between the rows of green. We put three candles in the field part and sang Happy Birthday to Cotton and then we held the cake up and let the wind blow out the candles.

We cut the cake and ate it while we talked about what we missed most about Cotton. Cason said he missed his smile and listening to him be silly, and Colt said he missed playing with Cotton and watching movies together. I missed snuggling with him, seeing the funny little faces he made, and everything else about him. Jordan said he missed him because Cotton was his favorite. He was joking, of course, but it always got a rise out of Colt and Cason.

When Cotton was alive, he was still too young to know what it meant to be the favorite, so when the boys would ask Jordan who his favorite was, he would always say Cotton.

We sat there on the tailgate of the truck for a while and told funny memories that we had of Cotton. We laughed so much that day and we celebrated the joy that Cotton brought to each of us. It was so good to hear those stories again. It was so good to know that

Cason and Colt could remember Cotton well. It was so good to have the family together again, even for only a moment.

I told the boys I hoped that every year we could come here to celebrate Cotton's life. Even though he isn't here any longer, we needed to remember to celebrate that he had been and that we were different people because we knew him.

I looked up and couldn't see the balloons and told the boys, "I think Cotton got his messages."

Colt immediately informed us that they had probably popped somewhere in space. Jordan said, "I think Cotton sat on them and popped them."

We all laughed. It was a good day.

After we finished, the boys chased rabbits while I cleaned up. Jordan and I sat there and watched our boys play. I told him that I was sorry that the party was so simple. He just sat there as quiet as ever and assured me that it was enough. We spent time to celebrate Cotton's life and not mourn him. We laughed and enjoyed each other. It was just as it should be.

೧೩ ೧೩ ೧೩

Days of joy and days of severe depression sprinkled my summer. Simple things like a song, a friend, or a memory could erupt in my mind as a wave of either grief or jubilation. It was, at times, a bit of a rollercoaster ride for me. My heart would even ache with joy or pain with the same thought or memory.

Days would be tempered with a tone of pain or even a haze of regret. Sometimes I would wake and attempt to be ready for the day, but the weight of my loss would be too great for me to shake. Days like these, my friends were so important. A date with a friend for a manicure, coffee, lunch, or just to talk at home could typically clear the clouds from my eyes and help me to function again. But as we neared the anniversary of Cotton's death, I found myself in a funk that couldn't even be lifted by a trip to the nail salon.

Sometimes even, if the fun trip with a friend didn't help me snap out of my daze, the routine of life would lull me back to normalcy. Laundry, groceries, cooking, cleaning, and chasing two wild boys could remind me of the fact that I am continuing to walk through this life with the strength of my Father. This was not one of those days.

At the supermarket, I collected the common and, at the same time, stupendous shopping list that I had compiled the night before. As I walked, I even added a few treats for Jordan and the boys, but continually felt the dull roar of sadness droning along in my head as I shopped.

A thud of pain neared my heart as I finally navigated my way to the check-out aisle. My eyes were immediately drawn to a family ahead of me. A mother stood there with her three children, waiting for their turn at the conveyer belt. The oldest was a son who was about nine years old and the next was a girl who couldn't have been more than six, but then I heard the little one call out to his mother as he attempted, ever so ferociously, to lift a package of pull-ups on to the belt.

"Mooooooooooooom!" He was working so hard to get that bag of pull-ups high enough, but simply couldn't make it happen.

"Mooooooooooooooommm!" His voice reminded me of how Cotton used to call to me as he tried to be a big boy like his brothers. He would call me with that same voice when he wanted to snuggle and I missed that sound.

I could hear Cotton for the first time in so long. Oh, how I missed him calling for me. The sound was both piercing and soothing at the same time. It was as though someone had captured a memory and asked this little boy to share it with me.

As the little boy turned around and looked at me, I smiled at him while trying to blink back the tears. He smiled back with the biggest smile. I laughed a little while my eyes filled with grief. I wiped the tears that had escaped and smiled again at this beautiful little boy who reminded me how good it felt to be a mom, but how much I had truly missed having Cotton with me.

Every time that little boy looked at me with that big smile, more tears flooded my eyes. I told myself this was not the place to break down, so I looked away from the little boy and focused on something else, but the tears seemed to keep coming.

I was so scared that someone would ask if I was okay, which would only free the dam of emotions that were being built up in my heart. Thankfully, no one did.

Soon, the sweet boy and family walked off and it was my turn to check out. I know my eyes had to have been red from rubbing them, but I smiled and chatted with the lady at the register as if nothing was wrong.

I muscled through the rest of my chores that day and finally made it to Vacation Bible School that evening at our church. Amazingly enough, the thought of being at church comforted me. It didn't free me from pain, but it helped to soften the sting. My boys had so much fun there and I loved being able to help.

The children got to use Cotton's playground and by the end of it, I was sure that God was present with me. Comforting me with the Holy Spirit and my church family. But the knowledge of what we would soon celebrate remained on my mind.

I know that dreadful day is coming and I'm not sure what to expect, but I do know that it will eventually be a memory like everything else and the only thing that will remain will be God's love and hope all around me.

One Year Later

Everyone told me that the one-year anniversary of Cotton's death would be the hardest of all. I have heard that from people who have lost someone close to them, as well as people who just say that because others say that. So for the last year, I've been dreading the one-year anniversary. My nerves tended to tighten the most over the week leading up to July 12th, and by the time it arrived, it was almost more than I could bear. All week long I was on the edge of an emotional break because I was told that I would break down.

But that breakdown never came.

I waited and waited for the crushing blow of grief to overtake my experience, but it never came. It never rose up and attacked me, and as the clouds began to clear, I began to realize that I had already made the decision that had set me free from guilt, shame, and sorrow. I had decided to live.

Yes, my son is gone, but feeling sorry for myself a year later makes no sense to me. Being told that I had already lost was more than frustrating. I was being conditioned to give up hope. I was being inspired to accept defeat, but my God is not defeated, and neither am I!

The last of the fog was lifted when I took a short little timeout to talk with the Lord. I found myself expressing to Him my trust for Him, my gratitude for His grace and mercy, and my resolution to serve Him. He immediately responded to me by delivering His perfect peace.

Colt and I wasted no time and changed the flowers

at Cotton's gravestone. I sat and told him how much I loved him and missed him. In that moment, as I shared my heart, I was reminded that the first anniversary is not the hardest day. I went through the hardest days when my baby left me a year ago. This day is only one day closer to getting to go home to Cotton and Jesus.

I used to be so afraid to die. It scared me. But now, now that I know where I'm going and know that I have a Father who loves me and a son that is waiting for me, it's not scary at all. I know that my time here on earth is for a purpose. I am here to be an ambassador for the Kingdom of God and I have been given a unique insight into how joyous it will be for us when we get there.

I have so much to do. I have people I want to serve and people I want to come to know Jesus so they too can come home to be with us. So they can meet this amazing little boy who inspires us all. I will go out and enjoy my family whom I have here, share the love of Jesus with everyone I can, even on that tragic day, and most importantly, I will praise God for the gifts that He gives us.

Yes, I cry and am sad because I miss the feeling of having Cotton with me. I miss getting to see him grow and hear his voice, but I won't sit and feel sorry for myself when I should rejoice because he has received the gift of being in the presence of Jesus.

He is there alive waiting for me. So how am I supposed to sit and feel sorry for myself when God has given us such a great gift? I won't be that person that sits and cries all day a year later on that tragic day because I feel sorry for my loss. Instead, I want to keep showing Cotton how much I love him and how much I remember him.

Colt and I finished up at the cemetery and got back to life. Our community has a program that distributes boxes of food to families here who can't afford to buy groceries. I went and helped with it for the first time. I got so much joy from serving people. It not only made me feel good to provide food, but it made all the difference in the world that they knew I was doing it because of my relationship with Jesus. It made food a representation of love and love was what Cotton gave me each day I had with him, not to mention the laughter and conversations I had with all the helpers. Serving others is what I want my life to be about, not how awful it is that Cotton is gone.

Satan attempted to have his moment in my mind and whispered his sinister lies into my ear. He tried to pull me away from God's love and support so that I would blame myself and be miserable. But with the power of Jesus Christ, Satan had no hold over me. I saw his lies and deceit and let God guide me though with love and joy just as He did one year ago.

I don't understand why so much focus was put on the anniversary when every day without my little boy is hard. I have to live with the accident daily, not just on that one day. I can choose to live a life under the weight of guilt and pain, or I can live it looking forward to the resurrection that Christ promised me.

I choose to live for Christ. I haven't forgotten about Cotton. I could never forget the tragedy of Cotton's passing, but the blessing and love that came from it is what I want everyone to remember. Not the pain and loss. No matter what day it is.

Gone, But Not Forgotten

Colt still asks for Cotton, but now understands he won't be coming home. We still talk about Cotton and how we loved him and how we will always miss him. Colt likes to talk to Cotton and blame Cotton when he messes something up. We sit together and watch the videos we have of Cotton, laughing and tearing up at the same time. We talk to our kids about how we miss him in our everyday lives, but we continue our days here so that he will be proud of us. We want to remember him for the beautiful and joy-filled child that he was. We want to miss him, but we also want to live our lives.

I remember how blessed I was that God chose me to be Cotton's mom and chose my family to show His power, love, and grace. Every day, I try to listen for God's guidance and do as I'm asked because I know following Him is the only way I will get through this life on earth and hold Cotton again. I am constantly reminded of the security of my own salvation and how I have been bought by the blood of Jesus. I have been called a daughter of the Most High God and Cotton was called a son. We will see each other again and we will share the joy of the Father as we are reunited in paradise.

Some nights, my dreams are so vivid. It is as though God sends Cotton home in my dreams. He says my name and comes running up to me and squeezes me as he always did. Cotton and I have had a great time together in our reunions. We snuggle and take pictures. Usually because I can't believe he is there with me, I just want to relish the moment so I sit and watch him play with Colt just like I did when he was still with us. Then, he looks up at me and I know it's time for him to go back. So, I hug him one more time and tell him I love him bunches and to come see me again.

When I wake up, I always thank God for that time with Cotton. I know that the pictures didn't really get taken, but just to have it feel so real was enough. I am reminded that the reunion of the dream pales in comparison to the reunification that will take place in Glory. I am grateful for the happiness of the dream, but I long for what is to come.

Other days are hard and I sometimes feel a pain upon my heart that is so heavy that it's hard to breathe. I trust in the relationship that God has given me with the Holy Spirit and I pray to Him for the strength to carry on. I know that He has brought me so far in my life, from a woman who fought against Him, to a woman who no longer needs to fight because the war is already won. These tiny battles are a chance for Him to prove to me once again that He is my provider and in Him alone I can place my trust.

On the days that are hard, I will pray, "God, I'm holding You to Your promises. You told me that you will call me home to be with You some day and that I will be there with You forever. I will live for You because You have bought me at the cost of Your Son. Show me that You can be trusted! Show me that You will never leave me."

It may seem weird to some people, but I have never felt as close to God as I did going through those weeks. When I remember those nights and all the tears that I cried, I remember feeling held. I remember feeling like my feet never touched the ground. I am amazed at the way the Lord embraced me and how He held me close. I never could have walked through so many of those moments. And to be honest, I didn't. He brought me through them. He picked me up and carried me. He carried us all, and as a result, I know the joy of following Jesus everyday.

My journey taught me to always keep my focus on God. It is the only way to overcome this life. Satan never stopped trying to take us and he still attacks me every day. He reminds me that I was the one who left the ladder in the pool that day and shows me the image of Cotton floating in the pool. He reminds me that I was the one who didn't do enough to save him; showing me images of me holding Cotton while Jordan did CPR. He tries to convince me that I am a horrible mother for not watching Cotton that day.

Even though some of those statements may be true, God forgave me, and somehow, I know Cotton does too. Satan is crafty at what he does. He reminds me of facts and implants thoughts of defeat. He shows me images of pain and destruction and tries to steal my joy, but my God is more powerful than his lie.

The truths of those moments are so much stronger than the lie. The truth is that this world is broken and our sin is what broke it. Sin demands that we die, but the death that we endure as believers is only temporary. Cotton is in such a better place that we cannot even comprehend it. Cotton is in a place where Satan's lies cannot invade.

I even think about how thankful I am that Satan can never attack him. God loves me and I know He paid the ultimate price for my salvation. So I allow myself to be forgiven. Because of God's power, love, and grace, I can tell Satan to leave me alone and that those perverted ideas are not who I am. The truth about me is that I am a sinner who was saved by grace. I was justified by the faith in Jesus' death and resurrection, adopted into the family of God the Father by His grace and love and am being sanctified throughout the life I continue to live.

I still have the passion of wanting to know more and learn more about what it means to follow Jesus, but it is different now. I want to know more not just for me. I want to share what I know with you. I want you to want to live for Christ and grieve with peace. I want you to know that it is okay to move on.

If you learn anything from my journey so far, I hope that a relationship with Jesus Christ is the most important thing you can ever have.

He gives us life and loves us through His church and many other ways. He uses our hard times to bless, not only us, but so many around us. When you are in fellowship with God through the Holy Spirit, you will notice his presence. And when you feel the brokenness of this world weighing down upon your shoulders, you can experience the freedom that is only offered through Christ Jesus. You can have joy instead of anger because our joy is built upon our eternal destination instead of the circumstances of this world.

You have to be willing to allow God to take away your pain, hurt, guilt, shame, and anger. If you hang on to those feelings, you cannot receive the healing touch of God. You must give it to God and ask Him to take these feelings from you. When Satan tries to put those feelings back into your heart by tempting you to doubt your Father, you pray to God and with His power, you can stand upon the victory that has already been won. Only through God will you have the power to move on.

How do you get to a point where you can do that? Here's my answer: Find a church where God's presence is flowing in and out of the people and learn to grow with God's people. Listen to the Holy Spirit and allow God to work through you to serve your local church. Finally, pray. Pray like your life depends on it, because it probably will some day. Pray like Jesus is in the room with you and allow your heart to be changed by your prayer.

My church family was a big part of why I didn't fall apart after Cotton passed away. With every visit to church, there is more love and strength from God's people, which helps get me through the next day or week. You have to focus on what God has to offer and not what you didn't get or what you lost. The hardest thing you will have to do is replace selfishness with humility and give all you have to the Lord. You will find that giving over control of your own life to God brings you the most amazing joy. A joy that nothing on this earth could ever bring. A joy that nothing on this earth could ever extinguish.

Near the completion of this book, Dannie and Jordan discovered that they were pregnant with their fourth child. God continues to pour His blessing into their lives.

About the Authors

God's blessing continues to be evident in the lives of Dannie and Jordan, as they grow their family with a new addition. Dannie shares her love for the Lord by serving at First Baptist Church, Ropesville in children's ministry, music, serving in the nursery, and any other work that God leads her to engage. Jordan and Dannie passionately pursue the Lord's direction in their lives and hope to share love, grace, and mercy to all whom they encounter. It is their desire that this book be a testimony of God's redemptive love for His people.

After publishing *Checklist Jesus: A Journey from Religion to Relationship* in 2013, Jeremy A. Walker prayerfully yielded to God's leading to co-author *Breaking Through the Clouds*. Serving as Associate Pastor to students and worship arts at First Baptist Church, Ropesville, Jeremy has been able to build a lasting relationship with the Greggs. After losing their son,

Cotton, the Lord used the simple gifts and limited experience that Jeremy had as an author to help the Greggs articulate the mercy and grace they felt from God as He heals their hearts.

Jeremy continues to serve his church and contributes regularly to Christian blogs, periodicals, and speaks at youth events all over the United States. Jeremy and his wife, Krystle, have one son, Rutledge.

Need additional copies?

To order more copies of

BREAKING THROUGH the *Clouds*

contact CertaPublishing.com

- ❒ Order online at: CertaPublishing.com/BreakingThroughTheClouds

- ❒ Call 855-77-CERTA or

- ❒ Email Info@CertaPublishing.com